RADIOACTIVE FLOURISHING

Radioactive Flourishing is for seekers of lasting happiness and peace. This book supplies cognitive insights for eventual behavioral stability. The USP of the book is its flipped human response toward instability. This book's primary goal is to help people learn ways to flourish individually despite being surrounded by instability.

This book is intentionally written in the "katha" style, which means that there are numerous relatable stories and a consistent journey from the core to the periphery, then to the tangent, and back. The implicit and explicit repetition of the key manifest enables the core intervening stimulation to encourage its readers to dig deeper and find solid footing in their flourishing being. This book is for seekers of happiness and peace.

This book is a must-read for those seeking to succeed in unstable environments. This book is for champions of happiness. this book is for those who want to be role-models of peace. It will also be an invaluable resource for aspiring leaders and students of life.

Arpan Yagnik is an ardent and committed student of Brahmavidya and Aatmagyaan. He is a consultant and coach of Fear and Creativity for Effective Leadership and Successful Management. Due to his unique expertise, he trains high-ranking generals and officers of the Army, the Navy, the Air Force, and commandants of special forces in Creative Leadership and Fear Management. He coaches individuals and leaders in Defeating Fear and living freely to actualize success.

Arpan Yagnik is a consultant, author of multiple books, columnist, TEDx Speaker, and a tenured faculty of Penn State University in the USA. His books are on Enhancing Creativity, Defeating Fear, Managing Instability, and Improving Intergenerational Harmony.

Arpan Yagnik was a Commissioner on the Pennsylvania Governor's Advisory Commission for Asian and Pacific Islander Affairs. He also served on the Erie Mayor's New American Council. He was the Convenor and Chair of the Global Youth Team for Initiatives of Change (IofC), which does work in 60 countries.

RADIOACTIVE FLOURISHING

An Innovative Approach to Perpetual Behavioral Enrichment

Arpan Yagnik

Routledge
Taylor & Francis Group
LONDON AND NEW YORK

First published 2025
by Routledge
4 Park Square, Milton Park, Abingdon, Oxon OX14 4RN

and by Routledge
605 Third Avenue, New York, NY 10158

Routledge is an imprint of the Taylor & Francis Group, an informa business

British Library Cataloguing-in-Publication Data
A catalogue record for this book is available from the British Library

ISBN: 978-1-032-62754-0 (hbk)
ISBN: 978-1-032-62755-7 (pbk)
ISBN: 978-1-032-62756-4 (ebk)

DOI: 10.4324/9781032627564

Typeset in Sabon
by SPi Technologies India Pvt Ltd (Straive)

i dedicate this to Ma Amba in Ambaji and to Hatkeshwar Mahadev in Vadnagar.
i dedicate this to my Mother, my Father, and my Sister (Chitra/Shailesh/Aastha).
i dedicate this to all my Gurus and Teachers, who have uplifted me into an existence of clarity.
Lastly, i dedicate this to the complete and absolute disenfranchisement of my i.

CONTENTS

ILLUSTRATIONS

Figures

Tables

PREFACE

Namaste

"The divine in me bows to the divine in you." i agree that saying this long line as a greeting every time you meet someone can be cumbersome. But that is definitely not the case with Namaste.

i want to share with you today why i support Namaste as a greeting of my choice. i am going to do so by explaining the inner meaning and deeper significance of this seemingly trivial greeting.

The first reason for why i support Namaste is that it is inherently respectful of the boundaries, personal space, and its related preferences. Namaste is a non-contact greeting. The differences in the boundaries based on gender, age, relation, stature, and wisdom are all well accounted for in the performance of namaste. You do not want to taunt a person's ego immediately upon meeting them by engaging in a greeting that crosses one or some of the boundaries.

Preferences pertaining to physical touch alter based on the place, time, and situation. Preferences can be explicitly expressed and made known to the other person. But that as we know, never really happens. Namaste is the perfect nullifier. It accounts for every complexity in meeting anyone known or unknown and greeting them... Be it boundaries, personal space needs, or preferences, Namaste nullifies them all. And this in the long run pays off because after all first impression is the last impression.

Talk the talk but also Walk the walk. Namaste is not just the talk; it is also the walk. Namaste is a combination of saying and doing. It is a performance that requires verbal and non-verbal forms of communication. An individual who talks the talk and walks the walk is assumed and expected to be devoid of conceit. Thus, Namaste symbolizes and indicates trustworthiness and humility.

The action of pressing your palms together slightly above your sternum and bowing down is not a submissive act. It is an equalizing act. It acknowledges that we are all integrations of the divine will. And we are all the same, despite the variance in our age, gender, stature, and wisdom, in our most reduced form. By doing Namaste it not only respects the other individual, but also respects and actually uplifts the greeter. i say so because the general human tendency tends to respect people who respect themselves.

None of you should practice Namaste just because Namaste is the oldest documented form of greeting that still exists among us. i myself don't. i do it because it is the best and the coolest way of greeting others and respecting everyone, including my own self. And to conclude this, i say to all of you my dear readers...

NAMASTE!

NOTE ON CERTAIN TERMS AND PHRASES

Unstability:

i have used in this book certain terms and phrases that are not grammatically accurate. For example, the word unstability. i am aware that the correct usage is instability or destabilizing. But i feel that the word unstability and unstabilizing comprehensively expresses the essence of what i want to communicate and hence i chose to stick with it.

i instead of I:

It is grammatically correct to write I when i want to refer to myself, but i find myself too insignificant in the grand narrative of the cosmos. Hence, i don't feel like referring to myself with a Capital i. i don't deserve a capital i. i have tried to retain i in as many places as possible. But there are some places where i had to give up because it is so painful and time-consuming to just have a small i due to my computer's wonderful need to correct everything that does not adhere to the already fed-in grammatical rules. It cannot handle the unstability really well and i want to be considerate in trying to not give the system any undue stress as it is ultimately helping me get radioactive flourishing to you.

Some other phrases:

i have used some other phrases in this book that you as a reader might be unfamiliar with. Some examples are Zone of Unawareness and Creative Psyche. These phrases are unique in nature. In many places the reader will be able to internalize them right away but in many other places the reader will feel the need to know its exact meaning and definition. Well, i don't have their exact meaning and definition. And even if i had the meanings and definitions, i would like to refrain from giving these plural ambiguity-laden notions a singular flavor. They are plural phrases, and their richness will only be depleted if tried and attempted to perceive precisely. Receive them and let your extrasensory mechanisms act to give them a space in your cognition or otherwise.

ACKNOWLEDGMENTS

i acknowledge the hand and grace of the divine in this project. i am glad that i could be an instrument for divine amusement.

i acknowledge my father's creative enthusiasm and dedication to transform the writing desk in our home into a clean, fresh, inspiring, dynamic, and a holy place for writing. Without these efforts, i don't think i would have been able to deliver my message with the clarity i am currently able to. A big thanks and my Pranaam to him. In the future at some point, i also want to write a book titled "My Father Is a Librarian." He is and has been the biggest champion of my work.

i also want to acknowledge Blasko Library in Erie, Lilley Library of Penn State Behrend, le café Marley in Paris, and many such spaces around the world for giving me a sanctuary to sit and an environment to write.

i acknowledge Amit and rest of the Routledge publishing team for their role, support, and faith in this otherwise personal and rather esoteric project.

i also want to acknowledge Lake Erie, Presque Isle, RSS Niagara, and the seagulls of Lake Erie for keeping me company during the writing of a big part of this book. Not to forget the magical leaves with the ability to change colors, and the clouds that passed above in myriad shapes, shades, forms, sizes, and densities.

1

WHAT IS THE 21ST CENTURY REALLY?

A critical understanding of the 21st century and what it has in store for us is foundational to the concept of Radioactive Flourishing. Also foundational to the concept of Radioactive Flourishing are many incidents and experiences throughout my life that have been incrementally sowing and nourishing the concept of Radioactive Flourishing. While i will share many of these, i want to start with one that i experienced in 2014.

Fair warning though that i will use numbers sparsely but when i do use them, i will use them with the sole purpose of relaying a particular sentiment and not to stun or sensationalize. i am going to make an active effort to not provide numbers or figures in this book. i feel that they do nothing more than momentarily stun the reader. i too have been stunned in the past, but i barely recollect any of it.

Water

In 2014, i was a fourth-year doctoral student at Bowling Green State University in Bowling Green, Ohio. Two major incidents happened during that time and neither struck to me as significant. But as i started conceptualizing Radioactive Flourishing, i was reminded of these two incidents and i immediately jotted them down as my second priority incidents in setting the stage for Radioactive Flourishing. i will start with the lesser priority incident first and then will introduce the higher priority one.

Anyone traveling to remote underdeveloped regions of Africa or Asia is prone to saying that despite being in the 21st century it is wise to not trust the

DOI: 10.4324/9781032627564-1

tap water in rural Africa or Asia. It could be contaminated and may even cause mild to serious health issues. This is understandable. Corruption, inadequate resources, absence of technology, and high pressure of population are commonly cited as the reasons for such misgivings. But i had not imagined that things such as don't trust the water that comes out of your tap would ever be said in a developed first world nation.

As i was working on my doctoral dissertation on Menstruation, i saw around me something unbelievable. On a fine summer day of 2014, all media outlets started buzzing feverishly alerting half a million people of the region that the water in your tap must not be used for any consumption-related purposes.[1] Not even brushing.

This is the region of the Great Lakes in the United States of America. The Great Lakes are the largest source of fresh water in the world. Toledo, which almost touches Detroit, is situated near the Southernmost Great Lake called Lake Erie. Harmful toxic algal blooms had infested Lake Erie, rendering the water source useless for consumption. These toxic algal blooms were caused due to agricultural run-off. It made the water so toxic that people were advised to not even touch it. This algal toxin was, unbelievably, immune to boiling as well. So boiled water too was harmful. The "no touch" order in the area persisted for three full days before it was lifted.

Half a million people left without water for three days in the developed world is also the reality of the 21st century. The people of this region continue to remain scared of the algal deposits that have become a frequent occurrence in summer. As if this crisis was not enough, another crisis was brewing to the North of Toledo in the city of Flint, Michigan. Flint has seen one of the worst public health crises, which compelled the then President of the United States to order a state of emergency in the region. In its efforts to secure cheaper water, the city of Flint decided to change sources. This change required the city to build new pipelines. Lead, which can cause learning disabilities and mental retardation, got introduced into the water supply due to major corrosion of these pipes.

Despite numerous complaints, the city authorities kept denying any occurrences of Lead poisoning for a while and did not act on the matter. They adopted what was referred to as a "wait-and-see" approach. Instead of acting immediately in such cases, the city stalled its response and eventually the city of Flint ended up violating the Safe Drinking Water Act. Fifteen parts per billion (ppb) of lead is the highest limit authorized by the Environmental Protection Agency (EPA). If lead is found to be more than this number in the drinking water, then the water source is in direct violation. When the lead content was measured in Flint, it came out to be 104 parts per billion. It was also discovered in the testing done by Virginia Tech that parts per billion had reached 13,200[2].

Water becomes hazardous waste when the lead content exceeds 5000 ppb. This was one of the long-running public health crises that the 21st century saw where thousands of Flint residents fell sick and suffered long-term health concerns.

All of this surprisingly happens very much in the first world. A major repercussion of such crises is that it has put the faith of people on tap water in the US on shaky grounds. i grew up in Ahmedabad, a big metro city in India. We had 24 hours of running water because our society had a bore well that directly brought us water from the ground. The Ahmedabad Municipal Corporation would provide us with water twice a day, which we used mainly for drinking purposes. This was before the introduction of water purifiers. Once they were introduced, we used water from the water purifier for drinking purposes. i had never directly drunk out of a tap till i was 25. We still don't do that in India unless the tap is a special outlet from an RO purifier. Come to think of it that even in this age and day we cannot entirely trust tap water in India even in the most civilized urban areas and never drink from it.

However, this was not the case in the US. In the US, people drank directly out of a tap. i still get my drinking water strictly out of my kitchen tap only but many in America drink water directly out of the bathroom tap as well. i cannot and am unable to drink from the bathroom tap but that's because of my mental blockage. Theoretically, there is no difference between the two waters. But i still cannot. However, after experiencing incidents of Toledo and Flint, i am not just wary of the tap water in Africa and Asia but also in America. This is also the opinion of many Americans because Toledo and Flint were not the only cities to experience water crisis. Since then, we have seen something or the other where people were left hanging without trustworthy and contamination-free water several times. Other issues included jet fuel-contaminated water in Hawaii; fire debris and ash in Las Vegas, Nevada; power outage-related contamination in Houston, Texas; high E-coli filled water in West Baltimore due to sewage or runoff; New York City public housing's tap water contained arsenic; and most recently the advisory in Jackson, Mississippi. Since such incidents are scattered, they don't get much traction in the national news, but when you put such incidents together you can clearly see the increase in the contaminated potable water-related issues all over the US.

Upmanu Lall through his research surmised that water quality violations have doubled between 1980 and 2015. And in 2016, water quality violations impacted nearly 21 million residents in the US.[3] Bottled water consumption is therefore consistently on the rise. While bottled water is much common and its per capita consumption is also high in many underdeveloped nations, seeing the same grow and rise in the developed world for the same reasons is alarming.

The two incidents (of Toledo and Flint) opened my eyes to the issues pertaining to potable water distrust around the world. The distrust is yet another similarity between people of the underdeveloped communities and the wealthy communities. When water distrust is mixed with water scarcity, the type and intensity of unstability it generates is incredibly radioactive. Water scarcity has always been an issue but what is unbelievable is that we are facing more and more of it now and are predicted to face much more of it going forward with the shrinkage of water sources. Most corporations are either buying clean water for their money-making ventures or are contaminating them for their money-making ventures. Both ways, they are not contributing positively to society in this regard. And now with the added variable of reliability of the water, it is becoming hard to quench thirst with a free and relaxed mind; UNICEF says that four billion people live in severe water scarcity for at least one month a year.[4] In India too, the Southern states have been competing and, in several cases, legally fighting battles for control of river waters. Water is a remarkable source of general as well as individual anxiety and radioactivity. This is really the 21st century.

Food

Moving from the topic of water, let me also touch upon the topic of food insecurity and its unavailability in the 21st century. In both the countries that i live in (the US and India), i have realized that in the last six years i have been living in a food desert. The availability of food easily within walking distance is simply not there in one country, whereas in the other one, the construction and infrastructural development that has taken place has cut us off from our nearest food sources forcing us to change destinations from where we secure our food and basic groceries. Despite me living in a mega city in India, where i should ideally be having a problem of choice of where and what to buy, i am facing a contrarian problem where my choices are restricted by the availability of whatever is made available by the new vendor who was never our family's choice of grocery vendor in the past two and a half decades.

i will use a number here because this has got to do with children, and children represent the future of our kind. Fifteen cents are needed to prevent severe acute malnutrition per child per day.[5] There are 671 million children in the world under the age of five[6]. Based on my own calculation it takes 100 million dollars every day to keep all the children of our planet away from severe acute malnutrition.

Fifteen cents doesn't seem like much, and neither does 100 million for preventing severe acute malnutrition but unequal distribution of resources, skewed geopolitical interests, and lackadaisical moral foundation have made meeting this number impossible. As i write this part of the book there are countless Somalian parents helplessly praying while watching their child slip into a stupor from which it will never wake up. Another way to look at a similarity is that infants don't survive due to high infant mortality rate in rural areas. And in urban areas couples don't want kids for lifestyle or other reasons. Both don't add up well in the overall equation.

It is believed that seeing your child die in front of your eyes is the most cruel, unfortunate, and destabilizing experience for a parent. Hundreds of thousands of Somalis are experiencing this misfortune every day as their children are unable to get enough nutrition due to the drought. This is also the unfortunate reality of the 21st century. Somalia for the longest time is the poster child of poverty, hunger, and all the other forms of not having. So, a drought in Somalia may not irk you much since you may be more than likely suffering from compassion fatigue for the Somalians. But then what about the Silicon Valley?

Displaced

Oakland, California is a city across the bridge from the silicon valley and San Francisco. It was a prosperous city where engineers who worked in the silicon valley lived. Now if you go to the website of the City of Oakland, you will see that the city is battling homelessness with an elevated emergency response. "Homelessness has doubled in the last 10 years. Driven by a housing crisis and continuing economic inequality that hits Oakland's most vulnerable."[7] Despite city's efforts the real number of homeless and the real reasons for homelessness are still not concretely known. Increased living costs, substance abuse, lay-offs, mental health degradation, broken families, abandonment, etc. are some of the common themes prevalent in these areas.

Acute homelessness has stretched government resources including fire, health, police, parks, and public works thin. They are unable to keep up with the sudden influx in the homeless population. How to handle or deal or manage a problem of this nature and scale is beyond the existing societal and structural intellectual capacity. Right next to where the highest number of ultra-high net worth individuals are concentrated, the rest are unable to put a roof over their head. To imagine that there are hundreds of thousands in developed first world nations without access to water, housing, sanitation, and other basic amenities is difficult. But if you care to know more about the 21st century you are bound to realize that there are more similarities about the dreaded and wretched aspects of life in these two worlds than one can believe or come to terms with. The homeless in Oakland have a much powerful and resource-rich system behind them so their probability to transition from their tents and streets to proper homes is much brighter than many others living across the globe.

Sadly, there are more and more people on this planet who are forced to live in transitional homes. Refugees' numbers due to war, civil unrest, ethnic cleansing, forced occupation, and more are out of the charts. Let me share a story from my visit to Florence, Italy. The story is about my interaction with one of such refugees. Interacting with him had touched me deeply but i was unable to really understand the depth or the radioactivity of the situation then. But now as i write about this concept of Radioactive Flourishing, it is vital that i share it. i share this because i am certain that it will stay with you much longer than any number or statistic, i give you. So here goes the story of being born on the wrong side as i wrote it in 2018.

> i love Florence a.k.a Firenze. It's my favorite city. It is home to the three Davids and the four prisoners who have been major highlights of my travels in the past three years. During my last year's travel, i was with a group of fabulous human beings who were soon going to have their first glimpse of the Duomo. The first sight of the Duomo is magical, and it leaves an imprint on you forever.
>
> i was toward the rear of the group and saw this one guy sheepishly approach some of the members of my group. He was of African descent and was trying to engage some of my group members in a conversation… Having been there, a few times, i knew exactly what he was doing there and what his next move was. The first thought that went through my mind was that this man is going to ruin these people's first experience of Duomo as he is going to thwart them and dupe them and cheat them. With the thought that i did not want my friends' first experience of seeing Duomo to be ruined, i decided to intervene. So, i walked fast, overtook some of them and jumped into the conversation to let all the others slip by and even nudged the few that were engaged by him to go, so then it was just me and this guy.
>
> Before i take the incident ahead, let me provide some background. There are a lot of these type of men in major tourist hotspots in Italy. Sadly, they are all of the African descent. They come to you, engage you in a conversation and immediately tie a bracelet or put a little tortoise or an elephant in your palm as a good luck charm. They do this giving part smoothly and swiftly while distracting you with their talk. After a banter lasting anywhere between few to several minutes, they invariably start asking for money. Money for that bracelet or the tortoise. This is when you feel cheated and fooled. But since you have spent so much time talking and since the bracelet or the tortoise is already with you, you also feel guilty. It's a trap and these guys are skillful trappers. They get you and they get you good.
>
> Coming back to the story, as this guy was talking to me and engaging me in all types of small talk. i asked him, why do you do this? The first time i asked this question it was mostly my ego and very little compassion

doing the talking. He maneuvered cleverly out of it and gave me the tortoise. Knowing fully well, what was coming next and being prepared to outwit and outsmart him, i took it. i asked him again, why do you do this? i asked this again backed by lots of ego and very little compassion. He did not answer me.

i kept asking him the same question. All i wanted was some response from him so that i could supply him with a solid rebuttal and say to him that what he does is essentially ruining everyone's experience. He should instead find something else more meaningful to do. i basically wanted to make him feel bad for what he was doing.

As i asked the same question the third and the fourth time, i myself started wondering, why does he do this? He kept talking about everything under the sun but responding to my question. And i was not paying attention to what he was saying but instead was engrossed in my own thinking land wondering why does he do this?

By the time it was the seventh time i asked him the question why do you do this? i realized there was more compassion and very little ego left in the question. And believe it or not he responded. i don't know if it was a response to the compassionate genuineness of the question or whether it was because it was the seventh time, and i was boring him to death.

He said to me, "brother i was born in such and such country in Africa. i was born in a tribe that was not liked by the majority and therefore i was hated. My existence was hated. They hated me so they did not let me finish school. They hated me so they did not let me gain meaningful employment. They hated me and their hatred threatened my existence. So, i left everything and ran. i ran, i walked, i swam. i was also on a boat and the boat captain also hated my presence on his boat because if he was caught illegally transporting me then he would be in trouble. Brother, i was hated everywhere."

"But somehow, brother, i was finally able to come to Italy. Here too i am hated. i cannot get a job because i don't have the right papers. And therefore, i do this. And for doing this the local police hates me; the local people hate me. Even the tourists hate me as i ruin their experience. Brother i am not welcome anywhere because i was born on the wrong side. Everywhere that i have been, i have been on the wrong side and for what fault of mine, i do not know."

His story and the accompanying realization floored me. i kept looking deep into his yellowing eyes trying to empathize with him and feel a little of what he had felt in his entire life. This was the moment of transformation for me. i never, like never, give money to people on the streets. Being from India, i have seen a ton of beggars or homeless folks and people in need. i have never given money. What stops me or what prevents me from doing so, i do not know. i know that i do have enough and parting with some of it is not going to make a difference. But i still don't know why i never give away money.

> However, my character made an exception that day in Florence. i dug deep into my pocket and took out all the cash i had (which may have not been an astronomical amount but still) and gave it to him. i also extended my hand to give him his tortoise back and he refused and said no brother, it is for you. i said thank you, but i don't want it. You keep it and use it to do what you do.

Globally, the World Bank estimates that over 100 million individuals are displaced. And displacement is highly radioactive. It makes a person frigid and scarred. His/her past is a constant source of nostalgia, the present is a source of dystopia, and the future is nothing but a nebulous dark hope. i live in Erie, Pennsylvania, which is one of the major refugee resettlement centers in the US. Refugees, mostly from Africa are brought here, taught certain skills including English and then are systematically introduced in the society. i had once attended a program in the Erie's Blasco Public Library. The guest speaker was Ansumana Gbembo.

Ansumana Gbembo was a local tailor in Erie, whose clothes were featured in the One World, One City exhibit. He was originally a refugee from Sierra Leone. He brought traditional African clothing to Erie. While he was happy to be in Erie and grateful to the US for giving him a chance at life, he sorely and dearly missed his home and his homeland. He was the son of a tribal chief there. People respected him back there. He was someone back there. Here, while he was alive, he was a misfit. He was an hourly daily wager here for a long time with no real respect. His resilience and positive attitude ensured his success in the American society. But he had some strong training from his past that had trained him to be a leader of men. He put it all to use and he clearly shone. But not every refugee has such training. He was also not pleased about the clubbing of different groups and tribes from similar or different parts of Africa. Such clubbing or stereotyping invariably happens during displacement. From an organizational point of view, it might make the filing system less cumbersome, but these people are so different from one another. They can't even understand the other person. They don't have the same traditions or customs. They don't even have similar clothing or music. Everything about them is different but their color of skin. And apparently there too there are clear distinctions, which are visible to a trained eye. People from some African regions are a much lighter shade of black, whereas others are a much darker shade of black.

Earth and Fire

While many are displaced due to conflicts, the planet will now start seeing a rise in displacement due to weather and changes in climate. The source of climate change is primarily anticipated as human and human industrial activities. Environmentally forced displaced will soon be the biggest reason for displacement. We are seeing some drastic changes in weather patterns. Let us quickly travel to the 21st-century California because Californians are living in prolonged droughts and there, they have water shortages. The situation is so dire that there are even penalties put in place for residents who abuse water for their gardens outside of the assigned days and hours. Well, there is another thing that is plaguing California and no, i don't mean to talk about the San Andreas fault line. i want to highlight the fires in California. In the last three years, there were 23,711 wildfires that burned down a total of 7.2 million acres of land and completely destroyed 15,448 structures.[8]

Other changes are seen in other parts of the planet. Ice cones in the Schwarzmooskogel Cave used to be 15 stories high. These magnificent natural giants are rapidly melting away into petty puddles. Similar disintegration of many natural, cultural, religious, and social constructs is a thing that characterizes the 21st century. We only got to know about these caves and the massive ice cones in 1999. But we have known about Gangotri for thousands of years. Gangotri is the mouth of the river Ganges. Tourists who visit this glacier for adventure reasons or religious reasons have noted that it is progressively retreating. We have known about Joshimath as a place for an equally long time but its popularity and place in history was sealed when Jagadguru Adi Shankaracharya established one of his Pithas here in the 8th century. Suddenly due to reasons yet unconfirmed but mostly believed to be pertaining to the insensitive and arrogant infrastructural developments, homes of Joshimath started developing cracks in them. Land subsidence has put homes at risk of sinking and the government had to proactively and under emergency situations vacate people from their homes in the brutally cold December and January months.

While the crisis in Joshimath can be averted by the Indian Government, there are many who are incapable of averting their crises because their crises are caused by others who refuse to cease their activities. Take Jakarta for example. It is the fastest sinking capital city in the world. The situation of ecological breakdown is so dire that the country has declared the creation of a new capital named Nusantara. Jakarta is the most populous island in the world and also serves as a capital for the ASEAN countries. Jakarta is not alone. Venice, i am sure you all have heard, is suffering due to sinking, increasing water levels, wakes from boats, and the pressure of tourist population. You may think that you can escape a low-lying region or a high-altitude region and shift somewhere else where things are more stable. It's a worthy thought. But how do you escape air pollution?

Air

There is no way one can escape air pollution unless one invests in a potent mask and a sophisticated air purifying machine that creates noise pollution and relies on electricity which is either generated by burning fossil fuels or damming a river. "The majority of the world's population continue to be exposed to levels of air pollution substantially above WHO Air Quality Guidelines and, as such, air pollution constitutes a major, and in many areas, increasing threat to public health."[9] i have spent the previous five months in New Delhi and Ahmedabad where the air quality is in dark red or some other unhappy and scary color. i could feel the negative and harsh impact of the polluted air on my throat and lungs. i could feel the difference because prior to New Delhi and Ahmedabad, i was in Erie, a city near Pittsburgh in Pennsylvania, USA where the air quality is in a happy green. How can you escape this menace?

Also, remarkably perplexing is when you learn that pollution is on a staggering rise in Sub-Saharan Africa, and Central and South-East Asia where a major chunk of folks, who cannot even afford a second meal, live. They are much more concerned about living today than suffering from bronchitis or lung cancer or smoker's lungs after a decade. And rightly so!

While the global South suffers from poor and hazardous air quality without proper availability of medical support, the incessant construction and mushrooming infrastructure projects in cities and towns have encapsulated the residents of the concrete civilization in dust. Microparticles of rubber from tires are also making their way into the respiratory tract of urban folks. And they too are contaminating us along with the ecology just as microplastics are.

Clean air, clean water, and unadulterated food are the basic needs of a human being. And surprisingly those who supposedly have access to these and those who don't are equally suffering from deficiencies. Deficiencies of vitamins and minerals have become prevalent in the haves and the have-nots. The similarity in the deficiencies is what excellently marks the 21st century.

As the old saying goes, "easier said than done." i do want to draw your attention to one more irony of the 21st century. One of the trademarks of this century is the ability to travel all around the world. Every place on the map is connected. With multiple ways of traveling, it has become easy, safe, and cheaper to travel around the world. In 1948, one year after India became independent, my grandfather's younger brother was admitted to the University of Nebraska in Omaha as a doctoral student. He shared with me that it took him 45 days on a ship to get from India to the US. He still very vividly recalled his first sight of the Golden Gate Bridge through which he ported at the San Francisco Bay. After that he took a train from San Francisco to Omaha. This journey added a couple of days to the total. i have travelled from New Jersey to New Delhi in 12 hours. While travel is easy and quick, a look at the US Department of State's website on travel advisories will advise you to effectively not travel to 70% of the places on the planet. See the map below to decide for yourself where to go and where not to go. The color of the US in the map represents the safe countries to go to https://travelmaps.state.gov/TSGMap/.

This is the side of the 21st century that stares at us openly, but we blatantly refuse to healthily accept or even acknowledge it. But what you have read thus far is only a teaser of what is the 21st century really. Let me use an excerpt from the 2023 Gates Notes here to strengthen my argument as well as to validate it.

> i can sum up the solution to climate change in two sentences: We need to eliminate global emissions of greenhouse gases by 2050. Extreme weather is already causing more suffering, and if we don't get to net-zero emissions, our grandchildren will grow up in a world that is dramatically worse off.
>
> i can sum up the challenge in two sentences: Getting to zero will be the hardest thing humans have ever done. We need to revolutionize the entire physical economy—how we make things, move around, produce electricity, grow food, and stay warm and cool—in less than three decades.[10]

i do wonder here, how humanity is going to achieve all that Mr. Gates is suggesting. For a moment, i say forget humanity, how is Mr. Gates, and the likes of him, going to achieve any of this? Because much of what he has done in his successful life has knowingly and unknowingly contributed to many of the maladies and sufferings. The computer revolution and now the electric revolution, how can we and they and you undo it, and abandon the past 500 years of industrial endeavors to instead come up with completely (yet) unknown ways of enhancing living standards? If progress and development, in their current myopic way, are what we seek then let's not even waste time by talking of achieving the stated goals. How is humanity going to eliminate global emissions? Despite the many potential promising solutions on the horizon to achieve any of what Bill Gates has said will not be possible until the entire humanity comes forward with conviction and dedication to let go of its greed and selfish passion. The need for radical and sustained contest of an individual with his or her or their own self is paramount. And this is what the 21st century is really.

Notes

1 https://greatlakes.org/2019/08/five-years-later-lessons-from-the-toledo-water-crisis/.
2 https://www.npr.org/sections/thetwo-way/2016/04/20/465545378/lead-laced-water-in-flint-a-step-by-step-look-at-the-makings-of-a-crisis, & http://flintwaterstudy.org/2015/08/hazardous-waste-levels-of-lead-found-in-a-flint-households-water/.
3 https://www.scientificamerican.com/article/a-growing-drinking-water-crisis-threatens-american-cities-and-towns/.
4 https://www.unicef.org/wash/water-scarcity.
5 https://www.nytimes.com/2023/01/18/opinion/famine-africa-drought-hunger.html.

6 https://ourworldindata.org/grapher/under-5-population.
7 https://www.oaklandca.gov/topics/oaklands-response-to-homelessness.
8 https://www.fire.ca.gov/incidents/2022/.
9 Shaddick, G., Thomas, M.L., Mudu, P. *et al.* Half the world's population are exposed to increasing air pollution. *npj Clim Atmos Sci* **3**, 23 (2020). https://doi.org/10.1038/s41612-020-0124-2.
10 https://www.gatesnotes.com/About-Bill-Gates/The-Year-Ahead-2023.

2
RADIOACTIVITY

Radioactivity is a process wherein a certain quantum of radiation is released spontaneously to shirk off and eschew inner unstability with the immediate goal to achieve stillness through stability. Radioactivity is typically understood in the context of the periodic table. But in this book humans are the context, especially individuals. The lessons and understandings of this chapter are to be applied to the context of humanity with individual as the unit of focus and emphasis.

Stable State

Water. Life came from water. Even after millions of years, water still sustains life. We know it and understand it innately. Hence, i will start to explain radioactivity with the example of water. Water can exist in any one of the three states of matter. i believe though that it is fair and safe to say that if energy does not act upon it, then the base state of matter for water is the liquid state. While i am trying to be as accurate and factually correct as far as the physics of this is concerned, i don't claim any expertise in it. So, if there is something technically incorrect or scientifically inaccurate, do not get hung up on semantics, know that this is only an example or an analogy. If this does not sit well with your cognitive functioning, move on to the next example. The point here is not to become radioactive about this.

As you come to think of it, water, diligently and consistently, tries to remain in liquid state. While remaining in the liquid state it also yearns to be still. When force acts on water, water loses its stillness, but it still does not lose its stability as a liquid state of matter. However, when heat energy leaves or acts on water, it reluctantly alters its state. In other words, it becomes

DOI: 10.4324/9781032627564-2

either a solid substance or a gaseous entity. For the sake of this book and understanding of radioactivity in this given context, i would refer to both these states of water as radioactive. In other words, a drastic deviation from its original still state. At the first opportunity, water will do whatever it can and needs to, in order to return to its original liquid state and moreover its still state. While it may exist in other states of being but water, in those states, continuously discharges its inner unstability to ultimately achieve its stability and stillness in the liquid form.

We humans too have a base state of being and existence. When irked or forced out of that zone of comfort, we start behaving differently. Whether we know it or not, we do so to eschew our inner unstability. We all invariably do whatever is needed to return to our original state of stability and stillness. Until this state of stability and stillness is achieved, we humans remain radioactive. We, humans, are constantly pulled from many directions making us unstable and subsequently radioactive. While a human possesses the ability to release and discharge energy in many forms to arrive closer to stability and stillness, the cost one has to pay to do so is not always worth it. Let me share two examples of radioactivity in humans around me and the subsequent radiation fallout from around my life. I hope that will help you understand radioactivity better. i will share countless examples over the course of the book so always keep in mind that if you don't like an example then move on. No need to become radioactive about it. i have already shared some examples with you in the first chapter. You can revisit them as you gain more clarity and understand them more deeply.

Example of Radioactivity in Humans

Generational Radioactivity

My family and i were visiting my sister. My sister's friends were also there. One evening as i went for my dinner, i noticed that my dear mother was annoyed and was at first muttering under her breath and then muttering out loud that why doesn't anybody arrive on time for dinner. Being the last one to join the dinner table that day, i was naturally responsible and also obliged to take a larger part of the blame for her annoyance.

Her annoyed behavior continued all throughout the dinner and so did her irate commentary about the lack of timeliness and discipline. She did not enjoy as much as she usually does during dinner and excused herself early. Noticing the prolonged disturbance, i went to her, apologized for my tardiness, and even pleaded to her in a light manner that she should forgive me for my tardiness if she can.

Despite my apology, her radioactivity kept emerging in the form of micro explosions from time to time. There was certainly something deeper that was keeping her from returning to her stable state. And for me this was a slight concern because my dear mother is one of the most stable elements i have encountered. So for her to be riled up, there must be some other contributing variable than just my tardiness from that day.

After observing her and enquiring with her in the next couple of days, i realized that she was unable to make peace with her realization of the apathy-filled demeanor of the younger generation. All her life, being the youngest in her family, she represented the younger generation but now she is unable to reconcile with the ways and attitudes of today's younger generation. What perturbed her the most is that neither my sister nor my sister's friend or her younger sister realized the need to help out in the kitchen in cooking the meal or setting up the table. Before you make the argument that why do only females have to help in the kitchen, let me clarify that i would have been equally in the doghouse for not helping, but since it was not our house i was spared for that particular instance.

My mother believes that as the host it is your responsibility to ensure that hygienic and freshly cooked food is served to the guests in a timely fashion. The apathy of those three toward the kitchen deeply troubled her. And to make things worse, they all did not show up on time, and i arrived super late. This made her radioactive. And to reverse her radioactive state back to being stable state, she kept exploding in small proportions with her jabs, curt responses, and lack of involvement.

Notably, in the same kitchen and subjected to the same situation was my sister's mother-in-law. She is much younger to my mother but compared to my sister and i, she is still from a generation above us. She noticed the same things and experienced the same things but the behavioral traits here in the form of apathy, tardiness, and shirking of responsibility did not make her radioactive. She was easily able to absorb this unstability, keep her calm, and flourish despite the radioactivity. How and why was she able to do what my dear mother was not able to are the two important questions.

You can write your thoughts as a response to the above questions.

____

____

____

____

____

Everyone Else is Inconsiderate but Me

Another example of radioactivity and subsequent explosion happened on a Sunday morning. i was reading a book when my sister came in and requested my help. i asked her what i could do for her. She said that the LPG cylinder is out of gas and that we need to get another one so that cooking could resume. i said, "Sure." We carried the empty cylinder to the depot where they sell replacement gas cylinders. As soon as we reached there my sister realized that she had forgotten a booklet that the gas company would need to process the request and provide a new cylinder.

Being a small village where everyone knows everyone, the merchant said, "Don't worry madam, i will give you a new cylinder, no problem. All I want you to do is go home, call this number and lodge a request on it." We got home, connected the cylinder, and the food prep was underway. My sister sat down and dialed the number to submit her request as suggested by the merchant. Her call was directed to a teleprompter that was giving her instructions. Just when she had gone a little further my mother entered the room eager to share the little misadventure she had. Between my mother's voice and the teleprompter, my sister was unable to hear the instructions of the teleprompter clearly. This made her instantly radioactive at that moment and she exploded.

She yelled rudely to shush everyone and went to say something to this effect that don't you all know that i am doing something important. i don't want unnecessary noise around me. This explosion came as a result of her inability to absorb her radioactivity and flourish.

i did not find her conduct proper, so i politely told her that her yelling was unwelcome and if she needed quiet then she should excuse herself from the room. At that moment she did not appreciate my suggestion and stomped out of the room.

When was the last time you stomped out of a room? What was the real reason for it?

You can write your response and thoughts below.

____

____

____

____

____

These are some examples of individuals becoming radioactive and then resorting to micro aggressions. Such micro-explosions are sadly becoming more and more common. And with the way the 21st century is moving, as seen in the first chapter, triggers that make individuals radioactive are on an incredible rise. Let me give you a few more examples.

Ignorance about the Body

Late in the night, one summer day, around 11 PM, i received a call from my friend. i answered and he asked me what i was doing. i replied just some writing. He said that he and our other friends had gathered and were hanging out and invited me to join. i yielded. When i reached the spot, i was greeted with an unexpected question. The question was, "Arpan, what are your thoughts about people who are able to locate hidden treasures using extra-sensory means?" Umm, now this was a rather curious question. i quickly retorted that while it could be possible, it may not always be real. I further added that gifted people who are more in sync with something either extra sensory or more powerfully attuned with a sense organ other than vision may be able to sense something that we are unable to under normal circumstances.

For me such conversations are important because they are opportunities to explore further what i know and don't know, and sometimes even upgrade my beliefs and knowledge. And i always approach such inquiries this way. However, in that situation that night, what became vividly evident to me was that there were three groups. One group who believed that this was possible. Second group that was convinced that this is not possible. And this second group had set out with an agenda to oust the first group. The third group was made up of floating electrons like me.

Suddenly, a heated exchange began between two of my friends who were obviously in different groups. One, using a lot of foul language, said to the other friend, "You have been rude all through out. You don't need to be rude. Enough of your tantrums. i can also be rude and there is no reason for me to take your crap."

In retort, the other friend, with assertion, said that,

> Look you have come in with a closed mind where you don't want to listen to or believe what i have to say. You have come here with the intention to prove me wrong or engage in a mockery of my beliefs. Maybe that is the reason why I am giving curt responses.

This tennis match of argument continued for the next five minutes with even more intensity. i was surprised to see how quickly things had escalated. i tried to mediate, saying there is no reason to yell at one another, and if someone is throwing tantrums or is misbehaving, which is out of character for the person, then maybe as friends we need to investigate if something is bothering that person and if we could do anything to help them.

The radiation fall-out was so intense that i failed miserably in bringing peace at that moment. They were both frantic. After maybe half an hour, i realized that all this escalated due to one suffering from a migraine and the second one from acidity. i also learned that they were both hungry. Either they had skipped their meal or had eaten less. Hunger mixed with bodily discomfort put them in a zone of instability where they both resorted to aggressive verbal behavior in their own intensities. None of us could understand the deeper reasons for instability and subsequent radioactive behavior.

Fifteen minutes later we all found ourselves gravitating toward a junk food restaurant where we all gorged on junk food in the middle of the night till our stomachs were full. Everything was fine before that, but everything became really really fine after that.

Have you caught yourself being "hangry" in the last six months? What was the most trivial thing that you overreacted to when in this state?

You can write your response and thoughts below.

____

____

____

____

____

When an individual releases a quantum of radiation, s/he might go back to a stable state but in that process, s/he rarely thinks of what the collateral damage is. The critical question that nobody usually asks in the process is how many other people due to my release have now become radioactive. Human society is continuously longing for stability. The billion-dollar question here is how secure this stability is, when each one of us is becoming radioactive. Radioactivity, especially human radioactivity, is critical to understand as it is directly related to flourishing. Flourishing is a mindset that is superior to surviving and thriving.

Radioactive flourishing is the art of befriending instability initially to ultimately developing the ability to absorb it. Although counter-intuitive, radioactive flourishing is the embracing of instability and moving in the direction of keeping a check on the collateral damage in the individual's surroundings. Radioactive flourishing is made possible by the absorption of the instability. A great symbol and example of radioactive flourishing is the great Mahadev Shiv Shankar.

Har Har Mahadev

A deadly poison by the name Halahal emerged during the churning of the great ocean. Many precious entities had emerged from the churning before the emergence of the deadly poison. All the previous entities were claimed by one or the other. However, when the deadly poison emerged, nobody volunteered.

The instability affiliated with the deadly poison was so much that even the thought of claiming it sent shivers down the spine of the entities involved in the churning process.

This is when the Lord Mahadev Shiv Shankar stepped in and consumed the deadly poison. We all are in one way or the other forced to consume deadly poisons every day. Poison here is merely a symbol of something that is unpleasant, that causes us grief and agony. Every day countless humans are faced with the choice of consuming their own brand of poison, which increases their instability. The central tenet here is what happens after the consumption of the poison. Who do we become and how do we behave?

After the consumption of Halahal, the deadly poison which could have wreaked havoc on the planet, i can barely imagine the instability that must have been generated within Lord Shiv. He must have the need and desire to spontaneously release radiation to achieve stability within him. His radioactive spills would have been devastating and far-reaching. The collateral damage would be unparalleled. Knowing this, he embraced his instability and even absorbed it to ensure that it does not impact others around him. He flourished despite being radioactively charged. We too must learn to step in and absorb instability to keep in mind the best interest of our *Srushti* (cosmos).

Asking a child and AI

As we learn more about radioactivity in this unique context something i urge my reader to keep in mind is that we all have a little potential to integrate and create something new. Alternatively, we are also always capable of disintegrating the already created. Both these abilities simultaneously exist within us. Being mindful of these in every moment of our living life is vital. While this may seem abstract at the moment, as we go further in the book, this will become clear.

Earlier in this chapter, i mentioned that radioactivity is a process wherein a certain quantum of radiation is released spontaneously to shirk off and eschew inner unstability to achieve stillness through stability, and that radioactivity is typically understood in the context of the periodic table. i now bring in a child and artificial intelligence to help us better understand radioactivity before we proceed.

American Corner in Ahmedabad, India, which is a part of US Department of State's sponsored program, had organized my talk on Creativity. In the audience i had the distinct pleasure of having a dozen or so brilliant children. These kids were super smart. They were also highly involved and engaged in what i had to say to them and the audiences. They had come with prepared questions, and they also asked questions about what i had shared during my talk. They were all part of a fabulous institute called SciknowTech.

During my talk i also spoke briefly about my ongoing project on Radioactive Flourishing. One student who must be 10 years was very curious and asked me how they could be a part of it. Well as it turns out, i provided two questions to that student of SciKnowTech through Dr. Megha Bhatt, who with her husband, Dr. Saleel Bhatt, runs SciKnowTech. i am including the responses of the wonderful and gifted child to better help us understand radioactivity and human radioactivity in the context of this book and from the point of view of the child and artificial intelligence. Thanks to Vivaan Shah for his initiative and eagerness to contribute.

1 What is Radioactivity?
Answer 1: Chemically speaking radioactivity is a process in which a material is formed in such a way that it releases radiation. This radiation is at such a high level that it can damage people, plants, and all life around it. An example of that is the bomb dropped on the city of Hiroshima in Japan by the United States of America. The sheer destructive power caused was most devastating and still there are many issues faced in that area because of the nuclear explosion. It has the ability to remove parts of the human genome. The TSara Bomba, the biggest nuclear weapon was 3300 times more powerful than the bomb dropped on Hiroshima. But biologically speaking radioactivity in humans is anger.

2 How do the principles of radioactivity apply to the behavior patterns of 21st-century individuals?
Answer 2: The basic principle of radioactivity is to reduce exposure and avoid contact as i said before I believe radioactivity in humans is anger. i believe the same precautions should be taken for both radioactivity and anger. Both are as dangerous as the other radioactivity is scarce and still causes devastation. Anger is everywhere, so imagine the damage it could cause everywhere.

When I asked the same two questions to Artificial Intelligence, these were its responses.

1 What is Radioactivity?
Answer 1: Radioactivity is the process by which unstable atomic nuclei lose energy by emitting radiation. This can occur in the form of particles (like alpha and beta particles) or electromagnetic waves (like gamma rays). The instability in the nucleus often arises from an imbalance in the number of protons and neutrons.

There are three main types of radiation:

1 **Alpha particles:** These consist of two protons and two neutrons, essentially a helium nucleus. They have low penetration power and can be stopped by paper or skin.
2 **Beta particles:** These are high-energy, high-speed electrons or positrons. They can penetrate more than alpha particles but can be blocked by materials like plastic or glass.
3 **Gamma rays:** These are high-energy electromagnetic waves. They are very penetrating and require dense materials, such as lead or several centimeters of concrete, to reduce their intensity.

Radioactivity can occur naturally, as in the decay of elements like uranium and radium, or it can be induced artificially in nuclear reactors or particle accelerators. The study of radioactivity has important applications in fields like medicine, energy production, and archaeology (like carbon dating).

2 How do the principles of radioactivity apply to the behavior patterns of 21st-century individuals?
Answer 2: The principles of radioactivity, while primarily rooted in nuclear physics, can metaphorically apply to the behavior patterns of individuals in the 21st century in several intriguing ways:

1. **Unpredictability and Change:** Just as radioactive decay is a random process with unpredictable timing, individuals today often face rapid and unpredictable changes in their lives—whether through technology, social dynamics, or global events. This uncertainty can lead to stress but also fosters adaptability and resilience.
2. **Energy and Influence:** Radioactive decay releases energy that can affect surrounding materials. Similarly, individuals can have varying levels of influence in their communities and networks. Some people radiate positivity and motivation, impacting those around them, while others may emit negativity or conflict.
3. **Decay and Renewal:** In radioactivity, unstable elements decay over time. In life, people often undergo phases of personal growth or transformation, shedding old habits or beliefs to make way for new ones. This cycle of decay and renewal is prevalent in modern society, particularly with shifts in values and lifestyles.
4. **Connections and Networks:** Just as radioactive materials can interact with and affect other substances, individuals in the 21st century are increasingly interconnected through social media and technology. These connections can amplify ideas and behaviors, much like radiation spreading through a material.
5. **Awareness and Safety:** Understanding radioactivity involves recognizing its risks and managing exposure. Similarly, awareness of mental health, social issues, and personal well-being has become crucial. People are more vigilant about managing their exposure to negativity, stress, and unhealthy environments.
6. **Transformation and Innovation:** Just as radioactive isotopes can transform into stable elements through decay, individuals and societies can evolve and innovate in response to challenges, leading to new solutions and advancements in various fields, including technology, culture, and environmental sustainability.

These metaphors illustrate how principles of radioactivity resonate with the complexities of human behavior and societal dynamics in the modern world.

Both Vivaan and artificial intelligence's responses are intriguing and push our understanding a bit further by opening doors of imagination and visualization. Humans are fully capable of radioactivity and radiation fallouts since they are innately desirous of stability and peace. All the skirmishes and wars and other heinous things are at the very core of it misguided and misinformed attempts to be stable and peaceful. It is very common to hear dictators and rulers that once i have destroyed all the dissenters then i will be able to execute my grand plan to bring forth peace and stability. Everyone in their own myopic and often radioactive way is trying desperately to restore stability and peace. This is not any different than water trying to come back to its natural liquid state.

We See so Little

How is a child expected to be able to admire and cherish the moon and the stars when they are hardly visible?
How is a child expected to be able to use her or his imagination to form new constellations and shapes in her or his mind by putting countless numbers of stars together?
How is a child expected to be able to see her or his favorite delicacies in the sky and go to bed thinking about them?
How is a child expected to be able to visualize his or her hero or heroine in the sky and go to bed thinking about that hero's courage and valor?
How is a child going to be amazed by the Milky Way?
How is a child going to fall asleep playing hide and seek with the moon?

Such questions inundate my mind, and at times they try hard to destabilize me and transform me into a radioactive being. This is one thing that does unsettle me. Honestly, for this, i don't mind being radioactive and even exploding because this is about kids and children.

We can see so little. So little of all that is out there. And that is what is heartbreaking to me. Every time i visited Ahmedabad, India in the last decade, i kept complaining that i rarely get to see a blue sky. The sky atop Ahmedabad is seldom a "sky blue," it's mostly dull smoky off-white. Yuck.

Urban population is on the rise globally. And along with it comes the push/need to stack people on top of one another due to a significant increase in urban population density. i want to bring attention to something that is disappearing fast and because of the substantial disappearance, it is also losing its relevance and meaning in our lives.

If you haven't guessed it, then i am referring to the Night Sky. The sudden emergence and appearance of the celestial objects in the sky is nothing short of a magical show. The twinkling of the stars, the shimmering of the constellations, and the enticing interplay between the sparsely populated white puffy clouds and the calmingly bright moon are nowadays hardly seen. The changing temperament of the clouds and with it the changing face of moon have excellent heuristic value for understanding the constancy of change and the cyclical nature of constancy. The disappearance of these has been disappointing me. And i feel really disheartened about it.

The ability to see the stars is a horizon-broadening mental activity. It inspires one to aim higher and reach farther. And now all of those inspirations have either disappeared or become nebulous. The feeling that you are not alone and the excitement of the possibility that there may be someone somewhere in those stars is never to be experienced in the city skies. And this I assume is adding to the already growing narcissism and self-centeredness of humans, which is a fertilizer for radioactivity.

The Night sky visibility stats are consistently plunging, which to my mind is an indicator of humans becoming more and more short-sighted. Take it one day at a time was a way of comforting and consoling a person who was shattered due to excessive grief or trauma related to a major loss in the family or an accident. But now taking one day at a time is sort of the new age mantra. If you have access to see what's 11 km ahead every day, i am certain your brain will develop the ability to keep and take the larger and wider picture into consideration before firing up the decision-making neural pathways. However, when it continually sees less than a kilometer on a regular basis it trains itself to consider less and less while making pertinent decisions.

i want to touch upon the impact of this on kids. Take a kid to a planetarium and the wow that that kid experiences is unparalleled. On the next day when the same kid comes out in the night, everything that she or he saw and observed in the planetarium is invisible or missing, obviously the kid is disappointed. Kids and skies share a unique and special bond. A bond that is essential during the formative years. A bond that may be short-lived but strong enough to sow seeds of nostalgia. A bond that is liberating and freeing. By means of urbanization-induced pollution from vehicles, constructions, etc. we have effectively eradicated the fuel for imagination. We have eradicated the night sky.

At a very personal level, the thought of the night sky brings back memories and nostalgia of the 20 or 30 of us sleeping on the terrace. The entire battalion of youngsters and elders sleeping in a line. All the aunts, cousins, and grandparents would be there sleeping under the night sky. And now such experiences that were a normal and routine part of lives are sold in the bazaar (market) as exclusive experiences in remote resorts for a premium which effectively discounts most of the society from experiencing it. The absence of night sky makes me radioactive.

Let me leave you with this thought that being in love with the night sky is fulfilling. It is undoubtedly exciting. There's never a dull moment. Because of our club membership with our solar system, we have been afforded a very nice seat on the edge of our galaxy. The view is priceless and what it does to you is indescribable. Thus, I encourage you to seek the night sky and experience its charming enigma and tender advances. If not for you, then do it for your babies because they deserve it.

Measuring Human Radioactivity

Measuring human radioactivity is not as easy because we do not have Geiger counters that can quickly tell us the amount of radioactivity, we have in us. Does that make measuring radioactivity in humans impossible? Not at all.

i have designed a simple 5-question Human Radioactivity Test (HRT) that will swiftly tell you if you are radioactive or not. All the questions need to be answered in Yes or No. If you have more than one No, then it means you are radioactive. The results of this test are not static. They are dynamic. They will change as you are susceptible to change. So do not rely on the result of this test for more than an hour. This test simply tells you whether you are radioactive or not in this given moment (Table 2.1).

This tool is cleverly designed because if you are really radioactive you will most likely not be able to go past the third question. You will be frustrated and leave the survey half-way. This is an indication that you must find a quiet place and reflect on what is the cause of instability and what can you change in you to be able to better absorb it.

Radioactivity within us manifests by disrupting some of the most basic of our functions. The above tool systematically covers each and every one of them and draws your attention to them.

The first question is about physical condition. Breathing is one of the most fundamental functions that keeps happening as long as we live. Disruption in our stability brings with it immediate disruption in breathing. When a person is radioactive their breathing is inept and their ability to regulate it is also deeply limited. When in a stable state we have the ability to slow our breathing or fasten it. We also have the ability to regulate the intake and outtake to a certain extent and within given limitations. So, the first question asks and

TABLE 2.1 Human Radioactivity Test (HRT) Questions

Human Radioactivity Test (HRT)			
No.	*Questions*	*Yes*	*No*
1	In the moment, are you able to regulate your breathing?		
2	In the moment, are you able to stand without moving in a stable position?		
3	In the moment, are you able to control your emotions and feelings?		
4	In the moment, are you able to solve a difficult puzzle?		
5	In the moment, have you lied in this test?		
Total			

Key: If you have answered yes in any of the questions, then you are radioactive.

tries to find out if the person has the mental balance required to regulate their breathing in the moment or not.

The second question is a key question. The hallmark of instability is the inability to remain physically stable. To sit in one position or to remain standing in one position is next to impossible while undergoing instability. This question asks you if you can stand in one position without moving. When an individual is restless, they cannot stand still. They will have an innate need to move because they are perturbed. There are two types of movements that one needs to keep in mind. The first one being walking where an individual moves from one spot to another. But there is a second type of movement which occurs while remaining in the same spot. Either of these qualifies as a No.

The third question is an obvious one. It is about emotional/psychological control. When unstable, it is uncommon to express a wide variety of emotions. We often get locked in one or two emotions or feelings only. These emotions or feelings take over our existence and do not allow an individual to experience any other emotion. Due to the hijacking of the self by these few emotions, the world and people become very black and white. We lost some of our discretion and discerning abilities. Neutrality is what one needs to feel. Too much happiness or extreme euphoria is also where you can't control your emotions. Everything looks fine because once again the ability to discern is lost.

The fourth question tests your patience. Solving puzzles requires patience in addition to a clear and unperturbed mind. It is extremely difficult to solve puzzles when you are unstable or are in a hurry or are in some kind of stress or duress. Even the thought of solving puzzles will make an individual who is radioactive explode. Puzzles are curious things which make you work harder than usual to get the same reward. A puzzle will require an individual to labor more and laboring more when one is radioactive is not really a priority making it extra challenging.

The fifth question is about ethical compromise. Ethical code of living and conducting oneself in the society is severely compromised when one is unstable. The lines of right and wrong, although there, become blurred and this reduces the natural hesitation and inhibition that one would experience otherwise. The presence of instability makes you cheat but the realization that you may have cheated will hopefully make you pause. If done in good faith, then this is a very good tool to identify that you are right now radioactive and you need to work on your own self rather than someone else. You need to work with yourself to find ways and means within you to absorb the radioactivity and move towards flourishing.

Something to keep in mind is that this instrument only tells you whether you are radioactive or not. Just as a thermometer cannot tell you what the reason for fever is, this instrument too cannot tell you why you are radioactive. This instrument can only tell you that you are radioactive or not. It is only through quiet reflection and introspection; you will be able to identify the correct reasons for radioactivity.

3

BIASES

Har Har Gange

i was sitting one evening at the bank of the holy river Ganges during the Aarti time. A typical practice toward the end of the aarti is to offer a lit diya (lamp) with some flowers and an incense stick to the holy river by setting it afloat in the river. The three are packed in a bowl-shaped structure by putting a few green leaves together. The moment when everyone lets go of their flower bundle is an immensely hopeful moment, where on the one hand a lot many wishes and desires for the self are being expressed and on the other hand there is the unsaid wish for the bowl with the lamp and flowers to remain afloat for a great distance.

i sat at a distance and observed that only some puja bowls would float for a long distance with the strong river current. To the dismay of many, there was a spot where most puja bowls would get caught in a swirl or start taking water in and drown.

Drawing a parallel from this visual, i realize that our lives are much like those floating puja bowls. We are put together with some ingredients to flow with the currents of life. Sadly, many get caught in the swirl and are either stuck there or start taking water in to ultimately drown. Radioactive flourishing is about empowering the self with buoyancy to remain afloat. It is through radioactive flourishing that one learns to avoid the swirls and repel water despite being in the water.

Biases and beliefs are two internal characteristics that ascertain your behavioral radioactivity. Interestingly, they both originate from and operate at different levels of awareness. The zone of unawareness is where a tremendous amount of activity pertaining to biases and beliefs transpires. Such activity

DOI: 10.4324/9781032627564-3

does not get registered consciously unless manifested through explicit actions or rhetoric. Biases and beliefs are of significance to us in this chapter. The interaction between biases and beliefs makes the foundation for many of our instabilities resulting in radioactive behaviors.

i want us to go back to the imagery of the Ganga aarti and the floating puja bowl. The puja bowl has flowers, a lit lamp, and an incense stick packed in a bowl made of leaves. Leaves are symbolic and represent beliefs. But there is one thing that isn't mentioned yet. The tiny twigs that are used to sew the leaves together. They are the essential ingredient responsible for the structural integrity of the puja bowl. They are symbolic of the biases that creep stealthily into and out of the zone of unawareness. Their interaction with beliefs as well as the external unstability, i.e., the strong current of Ganga and the tiny waves and swirls. These all are symbolic of the 21st century, uncertain and volatile in nature, and continuously challenging the stability of the bowl.

Think about what control does the tiny puja bowl have on the current of the mighty Ganga. It is barely holding its own, unbeknownst of the next assault of unstability that may just add a drop or two of water and tilt the balance against the puja bowl. Even a single drop of water is sufficient for compromising the stability and making not just the puja bowl but also an individual radioactive. A teacher of mine used to ask us, "how much percentage water is there in our body?" We would all enthusiastically think or vocalize 60%. He would acknowledge the response and say, "Well do you think that if I added a drop or two in your body, would it make too much of a difference?" We would nod our heads and say no, not at all. To this he would retort, "even one extra drop of water can bring you immense restlessness. i will tell you how. Imagine that you have gone to take a bath and when you come out, one drop of water has somehow managed to enter into your ear. This one drop will make you miserable. It will make you restless. You will not be at peace until you have succeeded in getting rid of that one extra drop of water."

What my teacher said made great sense. In the context of this book, the unstability of one extra drop in your ear is sufficient to make you radioactive. Whether it is a child or a homemaker or a CEO or a President or an ascetic, the unstability from one extra drop of water will make you radioactive. And your radioactivity will most likely result in a radiation leak or a fallout to revert to your original stable state.

Zone of Unawareness

Everyone vigorously desires to be stable. However, the sharp tectonic movements in the zone of unawareness are where the real game is played, which leads to your stability getting compromised. Biases are nothing but the outcomes of these tectonic movements in the zone of unawareness. Biases influence and dictate our radioactivity or in other words the movement away from stability. Their absence is preferable for radioactive flourishing. But how can we be aware of the unaware is what we want to try and wrestle with in this chapter. Easier said than done but to move from explosive survival to delightful flourishing this is an imperative step.

The cosmos we are a part of and our natural environment immediately surrounding us are highly and intrinsically contested spaces. At any given point in time and space there are entities pitted against each other for the sake of a little extra time in this constant race toward disintegration. The disintegration of the mortal form is a prerequisite for the ultimate integration with the cosmic timelessness is what we often fail to fully grasp. Time is going to engulf everyone and everything without any bias. Who comes in first and who comes in last is of no relevance or significance to time. Nature is a minion of time doing its bidding unquestionably. However, there is a speed breaker in the way of nature, which goes by the alias of Mexican Standoff.

Mexican standoff is a popular phrase for any situation where none of the parties involved can be declared a clear winner. In other words, a situation where there cannot be any further opportunity of movement or progress is a Mexican standoff. Another word for Mexican standoff is a deadlock or a stalemate. Superiority through sheer force typically or some form of lower-level intelligence is how plants, animals, and insects break deadlocks. Deadlocks are fairly common in human existence as well. However, as humanity became more and more civilized it resorted to less and less brute force for circumventing stalemates. Violence has been consistently shamed and shunned by the human world. It does not mean that humanity has eliminated it from its ethos or its practice. Humans are the only living entity that spend most of resources in building more and more sophisticated means of harming and killing others. Thankfully it has abstained from using the means of mass destruction and annihilation against others barring one or two incidents. From one point of view, unfortunately, these stalemates and deadlocks are of little use to anyone because they inhibit movement and progress. And when force was removed more or less from the equation then there had to be something else that had to come into play to break the stalemate, not necessarily end the conflict. This is where biases started emerging from the zone of unawareness. They are quiet, result-oriented, and excellent in fooling their host. Biases are the beautiful tiebreakers of the natural and human world. i even find it safe to argue that nature is biased toward movement, which can be faultily be referred to as progress and hence it circumvents stalemates with biases.

Without biases progress, good or bad, is challenging. Biases play fun tricks on a human mind and help it make a choice. Biases figuratively lurk in the zone of unawareness and come to the fore in the form of a thought first and then a decision or an action. What is also prevalent in the zone of unawareness is the knowledge of how they are formed.

Why do you favor one person more than another? Why do you favor one outcome over another? Well, one answer is that this preference of one over another is ultimately in favor of forward movement. These favoring dispositions did not matter much in a certain type of unevolved existence. But now that humanity has evolved, it has started developing a perspective and a point-of-view towards biases. Value judgments have been now ascribed to the momentum. Some biases are good, and some are bad. Some biases have led to the systematic oppression of individuals, and some have led to the systematic oppression of communities.

What happens in this zone of unawareness is something that we clearly don't have the ability to entirely understand. The zone of unawareness is like the modern-day smart speakers that we commonly find in homes these days such as Amazon's Alexa or Google's hey Google. They remain hidden in plain sight by merging with the background. These smart devices are always listening. They are extremely sensitive and keep capturing any and every sound that is generated in their surroundings. While they promptly respond to our queries, we have no idea how they are processing everything that they have been listening to while remaining inconspicuous.

Similarly, our zone of unawareness is not a passive entity. It is an amazingly active entity, but we do not know what sorts and kinds of analyses happen in it. What is certain is that the zone of unawareness is an amazingly active entity. It keeps receiving and perceiving all the time. The perceiving happens through the medium of the five senses. But then there is also the receiving, which is not through the medium of the five senses. There is a strong probability of receiving that supersedes and goes beyond the five senses. The extrasensory means of receiving and our lack of understanding the simple or complex analyses, interpretations, and resulting outcomes is why i refer to the zone of unawareness as a black box, where we do not have a complete picture of what is inside. One of the ways in which the zone of unawareness manifests itself is through biases. As i said the zone of unawareness is always receiving and perceiving. The zone of unawareness continually processes inputs and transforms them into instincts that become the basis of our behaviors. Our instincts supply us with guidance oftentimes before our senses kick in. But we are ill-equipped to identify and rely on such guidance.

Imagine that you are in an examination hall. You have to answer 150 multiple-choice questions in 120 minutes. It is an important examination for your future because it determines whether you are able to get into the stream of your choice or not. Here you have less than a minute to answer every question. In such situations there are always some questions that challenge you. When you look at the question and the answer choices, you sense that an answer is being presented to you from somewhere very deep within you. You have no idea how this suggestion came about but you sense its presence. There is a back and forth between your brain regarding whether you should trust it and select it or go through the calculations. Bear with me that this happens mostly when you are unsure of the answer. Like me, most of you also ultimately did not go with the answer that came to you and instead went with another one that you (mis)calculated. It is only after stepping out of the examination hall, meeting your friends, and comparing the answers you realized that you should have trusted the answer that came to you from within and not the one that your brain made you choose by overriding the previous answer.

Hasn't this or something similar happened with you?
Haven't you been told by teachers and wise people so nonchalantly to always trust your gut?

Isn't this being suggested to you when you undergo certain types of trainings? In the Western world, something that is often told to girls is that if it feels wrong then it is wrong. Don't question your gut. Don't question your instinct. They say so because there is a historical trend of suppressing and overruling the messages sent from your gut.

What is commonly referred to as the gut feeling or gut instinct is also a part of the zone of unawareness. i have several times made the mistake of not trusting the answer that my core being of existence suggested and lost points because of it not just in an examination but also in life. Our inability to identify and rely entirely on such messages is intriguing as well as unfortunate. i believe that this is the price we paid for our evolution.

My other theory is that we are somewhere in between evolution where we are shifting from our gut to our brain and hence are unable to give supreme priority to one over the other. i strongly feel that ultimately, we will shift toward giving one the supreme priority, regardless of the consequences, because nature does not like stalemates, and it keeps working silently to ensure that they don't happen and even if they do happen, they are resolved rapidly.

The Good, the Bad, and the Ugly

Biases may have their source in the zone of unawareness, but their origin is the multiple external stimuli. It can be argued that a child who is just born is free of biases. i find that to a large extent a newborn is devoid of biases that can be known and perceived through senses. But even a child is not devoid of biases that are received through means other than senses. To extend this line of argument, one needs to keep in mind that it is not impossible that a newborn may have picked up on stimuli that may have been received post conception via non-sensory means.

The Black Box type nature of biases makes them interesting for radioactivity. When something is entirely known then it can be managed. But since the origin, source, and synthesis of these dispositions are not entirely known their roles in instigating radioactivity are noteworthy.

i have benefitted greatly from biases. In particular, the bias that people hold in favor of my parents is the one that has benefitted me tremendously. All of my family, extended family, and even distant relatives have a fondness and a liking for my parents. It is fair to say that they are all favorably disposed towards either my mother or my father or both. Some of the reasons why my relatives have a bias toward my parents could be that both my mother and father are the youngest siblings in their respective households. They both have an amiable personality and due to their mature and neutral conduct they are liked a lot by people all around. Their behavior and conduct have been time tested, whereas mine is not time tested yet. This is because i have not lived as long as them and i also have not been exposed to the situations and circumstances that they have had to go through. But their conduct and favorability has deeply impacted my prospects and likeability in the society.

Many relatives who don't really know me instantly like me and are willing to help me because they like my parents. Doors open just because i am the son of my mother and father. People's bias toward my parents has knowingly or unknowingly (mostly unknowingly) aided them in deciding in my favor. To add more fuel to the fire, i look very much like my mother and my voice sounds exactly like that of my father. This relatability further instigates the bias. And i certainly get more opportunities at making my life easy and comfortable than others. i can't tell for sure because i have not studied this systematically, but i feel like i have also been granted forgiveness easily and grace willingly.

i have also received many academic invitations because i am the advisee of my advisor. It is my advisor's decades of hard work and rigorous scholarship that i am benefitting from. Similarly, the university that i work for is also liked and respected worldwide by many. This is yet another bias that works in my favor. While i have not done much for the university yet because i am relatively new there, it is the hard work and rigorous research that has happened in over 150 years that has generated a favorable disposition, which i am benefitting from. My sincere hope and humble goal are to do something that the favorable disposition intensifies and generations to come benefit from the same bias that i have benefitted from.

While i have benefitted from biases, i have also been on the other side of the spectrum where i was mistreated, prejudiced and unfairly treated due to biases. In 2012, i was among the few students who were funded and invited to attend a very special invite-only talk by the legendary Gloria Steinem—she is phenomenal. For those who may not know her, Gloria Steinem is the founder and the most prominent face and voice of the Feminist movement. During her talk she spoke of equality in the most mature and wise way. It was very clear to me that she is a legend. i was elated to be there and listened to each and every word she said with rapt attention. As soon as she completed, i got in the line like so many others to meet her. Finally, after waiting patiently, my turn came. i shook her hands and told her the basic obligatory things such as it was an honor to be in her presence and that her talk was amazing. But i had done my homework before going to this event, so i asked her about her two years in New Delhi, immediately after her undergraduate degree. She was then working with and for the upliftment of prostitutes and victims of sex trafficking. Her eyes gleamed and she shared some insights from her time there. Our conversation lasted longer than an average handshake and you are my inspiration type of conversation. We may have spoken for two minutes. She said that she was glad that i had done my homework before coming to meet her and she thanked me and turned the other way to meet with other people who also wanted to meet and greet her. i was on cloud nine. i had met a wise person, an enlightened person that had done so much for others. For me it was even more special because i was then doing my doctoral dissertation on menstruation and menstrual taboo.

While in a dreamy state of disbelief that i had just met Gloria Steinem, i noticed from the side of my eye someone approaching me. Before i could fully come back to my senses, i was being mercilessly yelled at, and these were the words, "Yooooouuuuuu... You all wife beaters don't belong here. Get lost and go back to your country." In the happy lucid state that i was, in the beginning, i couldn't even make sense of the words, but i knew something was off because my cheeks and ears suddenly felt really warm. My core, my instinct was reacting to the verbal assault. My mind took a while to fathom it and react cognitively to it. Once in my senses, i immediately responded by saying, "i am sorry for whatever your experiences have been, but it is not right to treat me like this because i have not done anything to you." This irate the person even more, and she started yelling even more loudly and saying that you all Indian doctors are wife beaters and that there is no place for you here so you should go back. One of my professors noticed my misery and instantly stepped in and shielded me from any further assault and embarrassment. Just because my professor shielded me, that woman launched a verbal attack against her as well. By then many people had gathered there, and i was safely removed away from the aggressor.

The bias that this person held against doctors of Indian origin due to her experience or understanding stimulated her to lash out at me. Her bias, which by then had become radioactive, had grown beyond her capacity to contain it and hence she exploded. Her radioactive explosion had left me unstable. My unstability was at its peak that night. The next morning, i had to go and share this destabilizing incident with my adviser. He counselled me and then took me to another professor. Together, they both helped me process the situation and initiate a positive process of absorbing my unstability. Thankfully, i had them both.

But it is likely that if i did not have them both or if i had decided to not approach them, i would still be living with that unstability. This unstability could become radioactive and could have manifested in the forms of micro-aggressions or a major explosion, which would not have been good for me or anyone whom i would have transferred the radioactivity to. The unstability is still within me but due to the receiving of proper guidance i was able to absorb the unstability. Despite being radioactive, i flourished. Moreover, i did everything in my power to not let this lone incident transform into a bias that i would hold against anyone. i am glad i retained my neutrality.

CBI

From a macro perspective, biases have become so massive that they have inspired systems and structures benefitting one set of individuals but are outright prejudiced against another set of individuals. As evolved entities, humans have identified some biases and initiated global movements to nullify these biases. For example, the bias favoring men over women in many aspects of work environment ranging from recruitment, salary, promotion, responsibility, and more.

Another bias that is causing radioactivity issues globally is what i would like to refer to as the bias for the familiar. There is an old saying that says "birds of same feather flock together." Humans have a bias to feel more comfortable and at peace when surrounded with people who are alike. This preference is extended to how the person looks, where the person's origins are, what the person's language is, and within a given language what accent are you using. Despite consciously embracing and adopting the values of pluralism and inclusivity, we, as humanity, have been unsuccessful in taking the familiarity bias entirely out of the equation.

Biases become discriminatory when they are cemented through policies and structures. Bias for the known and the understood is yet another bias which causes catastrophic divides between people, their opinions, and their actions. An unfavorable disposition prevails for everyone and everything that cannot be known, understood, and explained. Once again, i say that despite embracing and adopting values of pluralism and inclusivity, we have not been able to remain unbiased toward knowledge that is not generated using a certain system of knowledge generation. An example of a genius who was biased against comes to my mind. The name of this genius is Ramanujan.

Ramanujan is one of the greatest minds of the 20th century. His mathematical prowess was way beyond comprehension, literally. The world lost a superstar sadly at the age of 32 but in those few decades he published close to 4000 theorems and was also a fellow of the Royal Society. The originality of his work was questioned and to make things worse Ramanujan did not always have a response that was convincing enough. This created controversy. When asked how he derived the results for his mathematical advancements and contributions, he would reply that formulas and complex content often revealed themselves to Ramanujan in his dreams. He was a devout devotee of his family Goddess, and for him, her grace manifested in the way of these complex calculations written by her hand while he was in his dream state.

The then prevailing biases (which had morphed into beliefs-more on beliefs in the next section) did not make it easy to accept such explanations. This dilemma and stalemate created unstability. This unstability eventually also became radioactive for some. From one point of view if you look at it then it becomes evident that biases help us resolve conflicts as they aid decision-making. Well, i think that they also give birth to conflicts, but they sure do play their silent part in breaking or preventing a stalemate situation. It is for an individual and the society as a whole to deliberate and determine which is better and which is not. Is a stalemate better or a conflict? Should we not make decisions because they can be influenced by our biases is a key question.

i encourage you to do this Comprehensive Bias Identification (CBI) exercise. You will need to set aside 25 minutes every day for this and this exercise ideally needs to be done for a week (Tables 3.1 and 3.2).

The journey of discovering biases that come to your aid in daily life is refreshing. Without these biases many decisions may not get made, and many stalemates may not get resolved. This too has the likely potential of resulting in unstability and radioactivity. Simpler terms for bias for both sides are likes and dislikes. However, they don't do much justice to the essence of bias.

Sanskrit language has two apt words for explaining the two ends of the spectrum of bias. The two terms are "*Raag*" and "*Dwesha.*" Raag and Dwesha are opposites. i was explained by my teacher that they are both subjective values imputed on people, things, situations, and values. Raag is a favorable disposition, whereas Dwesha is an unfavorable disposition. i feel that the subjective imputing happens in, what i earlier referred to as, the zone

TABLE 3.1 CBI Part 1

Day	*Make a list of all the decisions you made smoothly today*	*Examine and list any bias/es that enabled you to decide*
Monday		
Tuesday		
Wednesday		
Thursday		
Friday		
Saturday		
Sunday		

TABLE 3.2 CBI Part 2

Day	*Make a list of all the Dilemma/ Stalemate you experienced today*	*Identify your bias/es that enabled you to decide*
Monday		
Tuesday		
Wednesday		
Thursday		
Friday		
Saturday		
Sunday		

of unawareness. Raag and Dwesha, my teacher further explained, are in essence the lack of knowledge, maturity, and understanding.

Imagine that you are invited to a marriage. When you get there, the people you naturally gravitate toward is due to your raag for them. And the relatives that you run away from is due to your Dwesha toward them. Such mental dispositions are formed, changed, and reformed over the years in the zone of unawareness in our minds and hearts. While we know much, we do not know everything that there is to know about it and hence i refer to it as the zone of unawareness. i reiterate that it is constantly receiving and perceiving. What is yet to be fully comprehended is the process that occurs in the zone of unawareness for organizing, analyzing, and interpreting the inputs for producing any form of actionable insight.

One of the subjects i teach at my university is advertising. i like teaching advertising because it involves exposure to a lot of creativity. However, this one thing my teacher said that has caused cognitive dissonance in me about teaching advertising is that “advertising is about cultivating Raag and Dwesha for others.” If you think about it, then it does make sense. It is only through advertising messages and content that manufacturers continually try to secure favorable dispositions for their products and services. While on the one hand i write and profess about neutrality (see my work on 5-Dimensional model for Faith-based governance), and on the other hand i am actively engaged in teaching young adults how to effectively lure potential buyers with the singular hope of cultivating favorable disposition toward the product or service that is offered.

Such dissonances, i am certain that you too shall face once the shining sword of knowledge and understanding falls upon you. My pride in teaching advertising has been diminished by this sword. And it is safe to say that my Raag toward advertising is slowly and surely reducing. i now think that advertising is unnecessarily extended to domains of life where it does more disservice than service. What i also wonder is how could something that so blatantly takes us away from the path of neutrality be so prevalent and pervasive. More concerning is that why do we even believe in it. Be it Raag or Dwesha, they are both equally away from neutrality. The greater concern is our widening distance from zero.

Now, i also go back to the question of what we should do with biases because they sure do have the potential and, in many cases, have led to increased unstability/radioactivity in behaviors of people. The bigger question that emerges here is that if there is radioactivity on both ends then which one is better than the other for an individual.

i want to reiterate here what the point of this book is. The macro argument here is that as an outcome of the path some have paved which the rest are willingly, and unwillingly following, the underlying uncertainty is increasing. This uncertainty will in one or the other way make us unstable, and subsequently radioactive explosions will have to transpire to bring down the unstability. The bottom line is that there is no escaping uncertainty and unstability. If that is the case, then we have to empower ourselves to absorb more unstability so that despite the radioactivity we flourish and do not continue to live a depleted empty existence.

With biases, as seen, there is unstability on both sides wherein there is unstability if a decision is not being made swiftly and there is unstability as a result of decisions being made based on biases. One way or the other unstability is going to be stimulated. Hence, there is no escaping unstability and the resulting radioactivity from it. Now the challenge in front of us is how do we reduce our radioactivity. By exploding, by channeling, or by absorbing? We will explore this further in a later chapter.

4

BELIEFS

Biases help us make a decision. Beliefs help us stick to that decision. While belief is individual, it can also be shared with a group of individuals. Belief is yet another manifestation of the Zone of unawareness. While biases are a bit more amenable to change, beliefs are less amenable to change. Correlating actions and thoughts with biases is not easy because many times the person is not aware of the bias that has developed within. Whereas beliefs are relatively easy to correlate with actions because the behavior of a person is very much in line with his or her or their beliefs.

When a person is not just aware of but also believes in something they behave accordingly. Let's assume that i believe in heaven and hell. And i am for whatever reason biased toward heaven then my actions will be in accordance with whatever will secure a reserved seat in heaven. We will circle back to the heavy beliefs of God, religion, heaven, hell, and more once we have understood beliefs a bit better.

i want to share with you a couple of my private conversations. These conversations are two decades old. Blessed that i am, i am still friends with these individuals. My purpose for using these private examples is to cultivate clarity about beliefs and how they influence one's life and exude beyond the self. Once we have a bit more clarity then i shall deconstruct beliefs and further elaborate its role in fueling radioactivity.

Digging up the Past

Once again, both these private conversations are two decades old when i was in college doing my undergraduate in Economics and Statistics. i have used

DOI: 10.4324/9781032627564-4

initials to protect the identities of my friends with whom i had these private conversations. The person marked as A is me. They have served as major eye-openers for me with regard to the incompleteness of my own comprehension about me, my beliefs, and my behavior. These conversations have stayed with me because they in their own unintended way prevented me from becoming radioactive in the long run. Secondly, their sanctity is also preserved without any exaggeration or degradation because they were handwritten conversations and i have preserved those pages. So, these conversations are as is. It's like reading someone else's text messages.

The first conversation is from 2003. My friend and i had met in college and struck a bond. She was impulsive and feisty. She was also intelligent, not from the marks and grades point of view but like in a street smartness type of way. We have not really communicated after college. i stayed in the same city, whereas she went on a different path in a different city. This conversation in its essence is a clash of beliefs. i will not give you too much background information. i want you all to make your own judgments based on your own biases and beliefs. i will discuss further after you have read this actual private hand-written conversation.

Conversation 1

A: Ok tell me why do you prefer N.V [non-veg food] to V [veg food]

R: I can't say why. It's just that along with dal rice roti & veg. (vegetables) I have another non-veg dish. It's the taste prob[ably].

A: Ok so nothing like everyone's eating so I'm eating.
Yes/No

R: ~~Yes~~/No

A: Ok! Tell me have u ever thought that what is our fundamental diet. Does ur mouth water when u see fruits, dal, roti, sweets, idli, samosa. But does it start watering when you see a rabbit, deer, a panda, a snake, ant, etc.
Yes/No

R: I can write yes or no. The animals you have named I don't eat, but in front of me if there is veg food & non-veg, I would go to the non-veg.

A: Ok then tell me why did people have to start eating N.V

R: I have no idea. I have been eating it since I was 1 year old and my religion does not say that it's a sin so I don't c [see] a prob[lem] in eating N.V

A: The people who started eating N.V were compelled to eat cause it was a question of their survival. The non-availability of veg. food. USA before 10 years was a total non-veg country but now after globalization, they get their vegetables in tins and u see the increase in the percentage of veg. people. In China, people eat rat & snake [be]cause u won't see a tree for 200 miles. So much barren it is. So non-availability is a reason. Is it the same with u?

R: It's not that. It's not that I don't eat any veg foods. It's along with veg that I eat N.V.

A: But I want u to eat only V & no N.V. i know that u eat veg food. What I want is that u quit N.V. Apart from the suitability of food, I'm not here to point out the -ve aspects of N.V but to stress only on the +ve aspects of veg food. If u want me to go on I will.

R: Everything has -ve and +ve. I have grown eating N.V. Me quitting N.V probably next 2 impossible. Its fine. I told u it's just not possible 2 convince me 2 eat veg.

A: Everything has +ve and -ve aspects but it is our moral duty to select that thing with less -ve and more +ve aspects.

R: I don't c any -ve aspects eating non-veg. So . . .
Moral of the story – I WIN hehehehe

A: u r so eager to win u will have to wait atleast 1 year for it. U don't see any -ve aspects because u have totally shut all the doors to let something against N.V go in. But at the end of the day when u say ur bedtime prayers think just think what is better? V or N.V. But first clear ur mind of all thoughts. Just ask for an answer from within that what is better because everything is good but what is better?

R: Ppl [people] have tried a lot for years now but all have failed & even if I think & pray my feelings or thoughts will never say no. I told u b4 [before] my religion does not say no to eat N.V So.???

A: Arey, I'm not talking about religion forget it cause its not worth talking abt it but it's just the selection of better to good. Why do u prefer X (a name was mentioned in the original conversation) to Y? both are good but someone is better. U r closing urself & u know that u r lying.

R: she is better (she chose Y who she was not at all fond of). no u said so. I don't lie.

A: The only thing is that u r not accepting defeat. Otherwise u have no logical & proper answer. If yes, I am eagerly awaiting.

R: I don't want to fight with u, u will lose I fear. & in the end that there is nothing wrong in eating N.V so I can continue to eat.

A: When did I say that there is something wrong, I already agreed to it yesterday that N.V for the sake of survival is accepted but N.V (Killing) for the sake of taste is what I don't like.

R: I don't mind it. I am not killing and god created birds n animals for us then why the prob. 1 life so enjoy it. I believe u should taste everything at least once in your entire life. LIVE LIFE KING SIZE.

A: if that is the case I don't think u have tasted liquid ammonia, cyanide or neurotoxins. Have U?
LIVE LIFE AMOEBA's SIZE

R: U donkey. Say sumthing tht makes sense. Not every damn thing can be tasted or eaten. I cant even pronounce these words 4get [forget] tasting them.

A: But u have already tasted them (animals) na one time. So then spare them and me and urself.
At the end of the day u r big loser. Couldn't meet XYZ, couldn't talk to that specs girl, didn't get the attendance, will have to give interview for the core. He He He Ha Ha Ha Ha u looser

R: Shut up & go 2 hell u LOOOOSER

A: That's why I'm here sitting with u, an all time looser

R: then go to MSc na. nyways all ur gfs r there

A: But I had also eaten a lot of N/V in the last birth so was unfortunately send to xyzabc & beside u.

R: go 2 hell stupid boy donkey monkey.

A: Tell me what do we do to a person who has died, to an animal which has died?

R: Animal, depending on which one it is I will eat it & person bury in.

A: Is ur stomach a cremation ground where u have to bury & decompose the dead remains of an animal which was ruthlessly killed and whose existence was ceased to nothing in 1 minute against its will.

R: Don't take load. I need 2 write my syllabus. Discuss(ion) 2 b continued until next time Buh Bye.

A: these lectures are as painful as laying an Ostrich's egg

i cringe every time i go through this conversation. i am sure you did too. Moreover, with the passage of time, i have noticed that i cringe a lot more than i used to because with time my sensitivities too have undergone change. So many things would not be communicated like we did by someone who is the same age now as we were back then. i hope you have read it and formed your own judgments and biases and what not. One thing that would be absolutely clear would be that i was trying to convince her to alter her beliefs. i had realized much later that what i was doing in that conversation was immature and foolish. But this conversation is something that has always remained with me as a means of learning.

Let me give you a bit more background to the conversation. i was born in a vegetarian family. i have grown up around people who only eat vegetarian food. i was born in a city and a state where a staggeringly large majority of people are vegetarians. My friends too were all vegetarian back then. This is the city where Mahatma Gandhi's Sabarmati Ashram is. So, when i went into college, it was a culture shock for me to be suddenly surrounded by so many people who were my friends that were consuming non-vegetarian food. i could not reconcile with the fact that she, who was my close friend then, was eating meat. Growing up, i always kept my distance from people who ate meat. There was Dwesha for meat-eaters. But now i had Raag for my friend and Dwesha for her one habit or lifestyle choice. Hence, as evident from the conversation, i tried my luck with my closest friend to persuade her to not eat meat. Well, she turned out to be the mightiest of all and did not budge at all. There were maybe a couple of moments in our conversation that lasted for days where she may have considered it, but such moments were fickle and few.

My learnings from the above conversation were that different people can have different beliefs. How could she not feel the misfortune of the animal that was killed and why did her religion say it was fine to consume birds and animals. These were things that my under-exposed brain could simply not wrap itself around. i realized and learned that behaviors are deeply rooted in beliefs, which are further rooted somewhere deeper—now i call that place the zone of unawareness. Neither did my friend nor did i know the origin or the genesis of our beliefs. But we both believed in these beliefs and lived according to it. i tried different logics and different ways to appeal to her, but she kept resorting to the two things that made unshakeable sense to her that i have eaten meat since i was a baby and that it is not wrong according to my religion to eat meat. Objectively, i was no different than her, and she was no different than i. Both were equally rigid. However, on second thought, she, i think now, was wiser than me and cared for me as a whole human, whereas i was, at least during those few days, fixated on her eating choices. And in that fixation, i may not have considered her as a whole human. i did not learn anything at that point, but i learned a lot later from this incident.

i now share with you the second conversation that taught me about beliefs. This happened in 2005 with another friend who i had met at a seven-day gathering. We developed a very strong bond of friendship and unlike the first one we are still in much more frequent touch today. And funnily i still have her phone no. memorized from 2005.

i was an ardent student of Economics then and an even more involved sportsperson. i was the captain of the men's volleyball team, and also a national-level university player. My entire worldview and thereof my beliefs too were formed by the learnings from the limited learning and knowledge i had of Economics and Sportsmanship. This conversation was a major eye-opener for me and remains one to date. It challenged me in the most loving and respectful manner and thankfully changed me as well. Again, i won't tell you much before, but i do encourage you to read it fully. Thankfully, i have been able to save these conversations because they were all written conversations and i'm grateful for that.

A: One very good thing in being conservative is that every single individual has been designated with a purpose and a task for each and every part of his or her life. So, if everyone keeps to their purpose and task everyone would be happy and gay.

Like men work and earn while women do the house chores and bring up the children. It's balanced. But when women step out, problems arise. I don't mean to say that women can't work. A woman has to work if her husband does not earn enough, but a woman should not work just to get away from her responsibilities towards her in-laws, her children and duties towards the house, which is adorned by her being there.

P: it's just our upbringing and socialization when we were children and were brought up to believe this. It is not necessary that every woman is happy doing housework and being in charge of the house. I'm not talking about those who choose to be housewives. It's perfectly all right if she doesn't want to work out of choice. But if she's ambitious and wants to engage herself in other arenas which will test her intellect at the far greater level it is unfair that she HAS to take on the duties. Being equal in a relationship must exist. She must be allowed to make her own choices and live life on her own terms rather than on those of society.

A: Yes, a woman should be given the fair chance and I have no hard feelings for that but at what cost? There are times in life when you can engage yourself in the activities you want but not in the years of life which you have to devote to your family. Because remaining away from the family increases the mentor pressure. Women are very soft at heart. They can survive all the endurance, but it shatters them internally which I don't like.

P: I understand what you're trying to say but my only message for you is women are not born as great cooks, mothers, wives. They are just the same as boys when they are born, and women are not always ekdum soft. Yes, they will always have to compromise, thanks to the social mentality.

So just clean up your perception of women. Give them more scope and accept their capacity of being capable and strong. No offense okay !! Just my strong belief and a sincere request. The woman is always made to feel guilty—the very question—"what cost" can be addressed to a boy/man also—but it isn't...

A: you don't get my point. All these are my beliefs and yes, I can be or may be wrong. But do you feel that I am a hypocrite and don't give woman a fair chance. Does this belief of mine deflect in my behavior? Tell me. I am ready to change and open to any good thing.

P: Not a hypocrite. You behave exactly in accordance with your beliefs, so you are not a hypocrite.

From what I have heard you talk; you have certain strong emotions about women in general. All I would like to say is don't assume stuff about them without knowing them for example all women love housework, that they are weak, less intelligent, etc. All these are stereotypes which a great percentage of the men in our society believe. Simply because we live in a patriarchal society where the man is the head of the family. I like you as someone who is very frank and has a great sense of humor. I'm telling you all this because I don't want you to be one of the several thousand men who have set notions. Just don't have these presumptions.

Give them a chance.

A: Women are neither week nor less intelligent, what I was saying is that in general they are soft but have a great resistance power which we (men) lack.

Another thing, I never assume or make any presumption, I go by facts.

Life is also a game, it's not a solo game it's a team game and everyone has their role to play and if someone goes out of his or her way the whole team will suffer. And I don't want people to suffer unnecessarily.

P: haa re baba, I am not saying she won't do anything at home. Just your attitude ya, I'm talking about. Bas. Now mind is going blank. Change of topic only if you have understood what I have tried to tell you so far.

The conversation continued, and maybe i will bring back the remaining conversation in another chapter but for this chapter this much is relevant. The above conversation was once again a clash of beliefs. In the previous conversation, i was actively trying to pursue my friend to adopt a new set of behaviors that aligned with my beliefs. Here that is not the case. We both were merely expressing what we believed in, and in that process my belief was challenged. The sport that i played extensively was Volleyball—a team game. If everyone did not do their part well then, the team would suffer. In my shortsightedness, i applied the same logic to society where what the roles were did not matter to me as long as everyone stuck to it. i am so glad i had these open conversations about my beliefs because ultimately, they allowed my beliefs to evolve and be more tolerant, inclusive, and pluralistic.

The Belief Wars

Beliefs allow you to stick to the biases and at times narrow-minded conclusions based on incomplete and inaccurate knowledge. By the way, beliefs are different from knowledge. Knowledge requires a solid footing in factuality and truthfulness, whereas beliefs only require presuppositions and evaluations. What is surprising to me is that knowledge, which is more reliable is prone to changing and evolving. Beliefs, on the contrary, are much more stable, static, and less prone to change. Beliefs can live on for generations. One belief that has continued to pass on from generation to generation for over millennia is that of the existence of heaven and hell. Another one is that of the existence of God. Different races and communities have, based on intuition, intelligence, experimentation, with assistance from substances, with direct connection with the said higher power, or through enlightenment have created notions and imaginations of God and passed in on to their next generations. Whether heaven and hell exist is a matter of belief. i am born in a Hindu brahmin family, and we believe in certain notions. The notions we believe in are much different from my two neighbors, one who is a Christian and another who is a Hindu but not a brahmin. i find this discrepancy perplexing and scary because it holds in it the seed of radioactivity.

My belief from two decades ago that a woman has superior resilience and endurance and is soft-hearted would have prevailed if i had not exposed it and made myself vulnerable. Even now i am risking greatly by sharing excerpts of my private conversation about my former beliefs. But unless we are willing to be vulnerable and be challenged at the level of our beliefs, we will continue to stick to our problematic and narrow version of belief and keep acting in accordance with it. i am here actively trying to eschew elemental exposure that can make me radioactive.

Because of my conversation with my friend and deep reflection, i now believe that what one eats is an expression of their choice and there is nothing good or bad, or right or wrong about it. There can be many considerations that inform one's food choices ranging from religious, moral, environmental, economic, social, habitat-based, availability-based, ethical, taste preferences, color preferences, health related, allergy sensitivity, lifestyle related, compassion based, and many many many more. To me it has stopped mattering what the basis of selection for food choice is, i know that it's a personal choice, and it must be respected and embraced whether it is in congruence with my belief or not.

Much of global upheaval has to do with enforcement and imposition of beliefs and belief systems. The winning and losing of empires, the colonizing of the world, the desperate desire to modernize the world, and many more have been nothing other than attempts to impose beliefs of the way how a society should run and be like. The two world wars, and the Cold War post that were all due to the need of a few powerful nations to make everyone else be like them. The familiarity bias was in play. They would feel secure if others too adopted their way of life. Their bias helped them decide and their belief in their way of life being optimal made them stick to it and keep fighting for decades.

Beliefs about religion and ways to achieve salvation have also resulted in tremendous loss of life and related devastation. Noteworthy here is that to believe and keep that belief to yourself is one thing. But the compulsive need to share that belief using different means, sometimes violent and sometimes non-violent, is what i find interesting from the radioactivity point of view. The clash of beliefs has the propensity to turn ugly quickly. i saw this firsthand at two separate instances in Ohio. Ohio is an agricultural state in the US. i was invited by a friend to attend the Sunday mass at a church. i was and still am very active in interfaith work, so it was not unusual for me to go to a place of worship that did not belong to my religion. One of the things that i saw in this church left me dumbstruck. Bear in mind that this is a church in rural Ohio. It is so rural that the kids over there dreamt of being able to visit Chicago or New York once in their lifetime. After the service was over there was a special presentation. A guy came and started giving a summary of the work that had happened in the previous couple of months.

The work that this guy was referring to was the work of giving belief to those who according to them had no belief. In other words, this was the work of giving God to the Godless Africans. This little church in the middle of nowhere on the world map was funding mission work in Africa. They were supporting six individuals who were in Africa giving God to the non-believers. And they took immense pride in doing so with grace and mercy and love and care as opposed to the others. i didn't know who the others were until they said in the end that they will need prayers for two of those six individuals because they were stranded in an area controlled by the others that were also engaged in the activities of giving God. The team had no contact with the stranded two and needed prayers for their well-being and safe return. Things got clear to me then that there were two groups with different belief systems that were contesting with each other to transfer their belief systems to these individuals in remote regions of vast continent of Africa where they had their own set of beliefs. Both the groups were trying that more and more people adopted their belief system. One was doing it with a display of love and care, whereas the second one was doing it with a display of guns and violence. My curiosity revolved around how much unstability and radioactivity this brings about.

Another incident is also from rural Ohio. A word of caution though that just because i witnessed these events in rural Ohio does not mean that they happen only in Ohio. Such events happen everywhere in the US, and they are fairly regular occurrences. As a member of the Not In Our Town (NIOT) steering team, we got an intimation alerting us to the arrival of someone with an alias of Brother Jed. Now i do not know the real name of this person or anyone from his family, and neither do i think that this was his real name. Brother Jed comes every year to university campuses and basically says the most obnoxious things. Things such as you are going to hell, and your soul will burn and be tormented in hell. All of this will happen because you belong to LGBTQ or have had premarital sex or have abandoned your faith. He and his family somehow are always able to gather an audience.

Every year students complain about this to the Dean of students and their professors. And every year they are being told the same story that everyone is entitled to their fundamental freedom of speech and these people also have the right to profess their religion. If your sentiments are getting hurt, then you stay away. They cannot chase you, but they are well within their right to say these things from the university-designated public space. Universities at times also have to arrange for police protection for these individuals because while they are incredibly trained to not involve themselves in a physical altercation, the students and other passersby are not.

Every year a new batch of students organizes a counter protest. University authorities will be reasoning with them, arguing with them, debating with them, and even transforming these moments into learning moments to convince them otherwise that every form of speech has a place in society and must be protected. It is a very interesting and an impressive display of logic and rationality.

Every time such things happen, it transforms the campus into a radioactive zone. But then there is also one thing that i have noticed that i must mention. At every such instance there are these over-enthusiastic one or two individuals who were the most vocal and involved in the counter-protest and arguing against the rhetoric through their logic, rationality, facts, and notions of truth. i have often seen them later in the evening having a one-on-one conversation with the family of Brother Jed in the most calm and careful manner. And later i would learn that it was the vehemently opposing ones who had surprisingly pledged their allegiance to the belief that they were so vehemently fighting against.

Such clash of beliefs has always fascinated me. Once i decided to inquire more about the hate-filled methodology of spreading a belief system. In one of my conversations with a Christian faith leader, i did get an insight. i was carefully told that one hammer does not work for all nails. Every nail requires a specific-sized hammer and a specific level of force for it to be nailed. Similarly, every supposed Godless individual also requires a unique approach and a specific force to recognize and adopt a new belief system. And this practice of saying obnoxious and unpleasant things is not new. It has been going on for centuries. It was easy for me to surmise that this was a successful proselytizing strategy because if something was going on for centuries then it had to yield results. No endeavor of humans has survived without results and success. If success is not a part of the equation, then the intelligent success-hungry human puts an end to that activity. So, the very fact that this way is alive and acted upon even in the 21st century means that this was something that was successful back in the 16th century and is also successful in the 21st century.

Something similar happens in my current university. A university student club invites controversial speakers who speak against certain groups openly without any consideration for their feelings. The controversial speakers speak what they firmly believe. Although they do not find much resonance from the population at large but their coming to the campus does surely create an unstable environment. To add fuel to the fire these controversial speakers are invited and paid handsomely using the money from the student funds allocated to the clubs. This angers students even more because they feel that their tuition dollars are being spent unfairly in paying these controversial speakers. Sadly, my university becomes unstable, and several minor behavioral explosions happen.

Many students even come to us to share their frustration, understand why university is not doing something about this situation, and more. The availability of mentors, advisers, and counseling center staff helps students absorb this unstability, sadly not entirely. i applaud the proactive efforts that Penn State University's President Bendapudi took this year at her end to enable students to absorb the radioactivity and not let it become explosive. i am sharing a link in the footnote to a 4:20 minutes video[1] by her that highlights the issue of controversial speakers, and the upholding of the constitution and role of public universities. This is again a clash of beliefs and from an institutional point of view, it has to play the role of protecting both the countering beliefs and the larger belief that free speech must be protected at all times.

If you come to think of it, there is also a hierarchy here in the beliefs. The controversial anachronistic beliefs of the controversial speakers against the LGBTQ community or women or minorities are at the lower level along with the non-controversial timely countering beliefs. While these beliefs are clashing feverishly and eventually one will gain dominance and the other will slowly fade away or survive in small pockets, the higher-level belief in the right to Free Speech is being upheld. The belief that Free Speech must be protected no matter what the cost is seen here live in action. Despite the disgruntlement and disappointment of a majority of student population, Free Speech of the minority students who believe differently is being protected and even supported. Hence, the belief in Free Speech is the higher-order belief system.

The above two are examples of how people actively and in many ways in an organized manner work to share and spread their belief systems. There is a particular congregation, rather an offshoot of Hindu religion, known as ISCKON where you see the believers distributing the Bhagvad Gita on the streets and singing and dancing. The singing and dancing are otherwise known as Kirtan. They invite and encourage you to join them in singing and dancing, which is also another way of spreading the message of what they believe in. All these take me back to my days of Federal Communications Commission (FCC) training for becoming a certified Radio DJ. While i was being trained to be a radio DJ, i was also teaching a course on global telecommunications. One of the themes that was consistent in both was the clash of airwaves. Every radio station wanted more and more reach for their airwaves so that they could reach a greater number of people. They would play mischiefs with one another and purchase devices with more power to spread the airwaves which would subdue the weaker ones. It is the same with beliefs.

Every belief is struggling and fighting for more and more believers. In the name of stability, their need to proliferate brings more unstability, individually and globally, which is problematic.

Ocean Agenda

The land that we live on is a very tiny proportion of all the land that exists on the planet. Our bias for what is known and familiar has created an unfavorable disposition toward the land that we have not yet become familiar with and know much about. This has given birth to certain beliefs that unknown and far-off lands are not safe and we must stay away from it. Well, because of this belief and bias, we know very little about land in the ocean. Agenda Ocean of the World Economic Forum is trying to diffuse the bias and the belief so that more resources and attention are dedicated to understanding and knowing more about what fundamentally the greater part of our planet is.

A large majority of land is buried under deep ocean. These are the largest masses of land on the entire planet, and we hardly know anything about them. They remain submerged with little to no light falling on them. Alan Jamieson points out that we keep propagating misnomers to people from a very young age that the deep sea is a horrible scary place that one should not go. The same is repeated and believed when further intensified and propagated by documentaries that explicitly state that deep sea is a cold dark alien place full of monsters. This belief has prevented us from knowing about the land mass that is fundamentally most of planet earth. He adds that it is pertinent that we must understand how we are impacting it and how does it work to better equip ourselves against any kind of disturbance or harm.

It is this bias against what is not familiar and belief that it is a scary place that has kept the population at large from thinking and dedicating mental and financial resources to this region. However, there is extensive use and abuse of this space for various purposes, and we all pay no attention to it. Concerning the most would be the mining of minerals that happen with little oversight. The freedom that one has in International Waters is not something that we have on land anywhere on the planet.

What is your belief about deep ocean? i hope you challenge it and confront it in the space below.

Your Belief:

____

____

____

How are you going to challenge your beliefs?

Note

1 https://www.psu.edu/news/administration/story/watch-president-bendapudi-addresses-controversial-speakers-visiting-penn-state/?utm_audience=Faculty&utm_source=newswire&utm_medium=email&utm_campaign=Penn%20State%20Today&utm_content=04-03-2023-21-01&utm_term=featured.

5

ANXIETY, FANTASY, AND INJUSTICE

An unbelievably large portion of human energy and resources is spent in grappling and juggling Anxiety, Fantasy, and Injustice. These three are incredibly destabilizing. And hence, a cause for much radioactivity in individuals. What Now, What If, and Why Not, from a radioactivity point of view, are symbols of Anxiety, Fantasy, and Injustice.

Anxiety, Fantasy, and Injustice lurk in the crevices patiently awaiting a reduction in psychic vitality. They remain undetected until they come into action. Even after coming into action, it is not necessary that they are instantly detected. It is only much after they are long gone that we fully realize that they sprinkled their fairy dust on us. They are invisible to you just like the many hundreds of insects and birds and animals are to you when you are passing through a forest. But it doesn't mean that they don't exist. Every time, i look at a calm waterbody i realize my smallness and insignificance in being able to perceive the vibrant presence of living and growing and moving beings under the calm water. Living, growing, and moving beings in enormous proportions are all there beneath the water, just the good thing is that they don't exclusively exist to get you, whereas the above three are out there to get you and bring instability in you. i wouldn't say that i have been a steady victim of these three questions but then at the same time it's not that i have been entirely immune to these questions either. i have been challenged by them at times, and on occasion or two, their impact led me to discharge radioactivity as well. i am not proud of those moments.

DOI: 10.4324/9781032627564-5

What Now (Anxiety)

When maturity, reasoning, and most importantly faith in oneself go on a hiatus, the What Now question comes to the fore. What Now is a question that emerges from some kind of inactive awaiting. Waiting is anyways painful. A peculiar thing that happens when you are waiting is that time slows down. A moment seems like a lifetime. The relative slowing of time instigates the formation of fault lines in our psychic vitality. Our Zone of unawareness has so many things in store that we are not entirely aware of or even understand. Many notions and thoughts that are usually trapped in our zone of unawareness suddenly surface. They come equipped with their own brands of armament and start attacking our already weakened psychic vitality. In normal circumstances, these thoughts and notions have no possibility of breaking through. But when our psychic vitality is at its peak vulnerability, it is not as strong as it fundamentally is, these thoughts break through.

The What Now question also arises when you have taken an action and have received an outcome of a subpar nature. One potent example is of the 10th and 12th standard board exams in India. The result of the 10th and 12th standard board exams is the critical make-or-break moment in the lives of most students and their families. i say so because this is when you determine what stream you will choose for studying further. Typically, students have three options to choose from, namely, the Science stream, the Commerce stream, and the Arts Stream. Nowadays the Science stream is divided into options of Life sciences for those who want to pursue medical science-related career options, and Physics and Mathematics for those who want to pursue Engineering-related career options. After the 12th standard board exams, you actually choose the bachelor's with a major in which you do your specialty.

Due to the massive number of students giving this exam every year, there are cutoffs and quotas. Each school and college require a certain percentage and if you obtain less then you will not get admission. India also has quotas wherein depending on the caste, gender, disability status, there are some seats that are reserved for you. Say you want to become a computer engineer and the cutoff for it is 87%. Now instead of 87% you obtained 85%, the What Now question comes into play. Suddenly all you had planned of doing cannot be put into effect, and since you were so focused on this one option that it is challenging to now start planning your life differently. For example, you had imagined that you were going to become a doctor and now you realize that you can only become an accountant in a bank. This is a major destabilizing time of the year and one can witness many radioactive explosions all around. The worst types of radioactive explosions are observed in the form of suicides. Many students because of their inability to visualize life alternatively or due to the self-inflicted stigma and shame of obtaining less marks feel unworthy and ultimately decide to end their lives. If you are an Indian reader reading this, then i am fairly certain that you would be aware of one or two cases around you where someone committed suicide because they either got less marks or failed.

When we carefully ponder, What Now is the question of Anxiety. And these questions come into our lives at every given opportunity. i am including below some examples of times when the What Now question appears.

- when you are rejected for a job,
- When you are rejected by your girlfriend,
- When you are terminated from the job
- When your garden does not flourish and flower the way you want
- When your car does not start or stops in between
- When the bank denies your loan application
- When you lose a dear one
- When you break the button of your favorite shirt right before an interview
- When you don't fit into a dress that you have earmarked for a special occasion
- When someone unfriends, unfollows, or blocks you on the internet
- When you lose your wallet
- When you lose your phone
- When you don't get your due promotion
- When you don't get an increment
- When you get an unfavorable diagnosis from your doctor
- When you are forced to move because of a war or a civil unrest
- When there is a burglary in your home, or your wallet is pickpocketed
- When the weather becomes unexpectedly violent, and you are trapped in it

In all the above situations, since the outcome is either subpar or unwanted the What Now question emerges, and along with it emerges anxiety. Although anxiety and stress are interchangeably used, they are substantially different. The difference between the two must be learned and understood well. Apart from stress and anxiety, there is also depression, which is somewhat of an extreme state of functional paralysis. We will concern ourselves here only with stress and anxiety, and mainly anxiety. Every day we experience countless stressful situations. These situations create a tension and/or inflammation in your system. Something noteworthy is that not all stress is bad. Some stress is good and needed for the expansion and growth of psychic vitality. However, things get serious when stress persists and starts impeding the regular functioning of an individual. Stress is usually about something that has happened. Anxiety is different. Anxiety is also connected to something that has happened, but it is more concerned with the future. What Now is short for What will I do now.

i lost my job, what will i do now? i have Cancer, what will i do now? My girlfriend rejected my marriage proposal, what will i do now? My loan was denied, what will i do now? i have failed my 12th exams, now i will not be able to be a doctor, what will i do now?

Anxiety is about the future, and it is our inability in the moment to fathom the alternate possibilities and solutions pertaining to our future. For those who cannot overcome their anxiety many times they even unfortunately and ultimately resort to ending their life. When your ability to see your life in future or in a certain design of future is compromised then anxiety grips you. And then there are moments when this inability overwhelms you and that is commonly known as panic attacks. In a normal state, one can visualize their future but when this ability is compromised and one cannot realize what will happen now, a sort of panic sets in. And in this state of panic breathing becomes irregular, heartbeat elevates, blood pressure is altered, and at times the feeling of disembodiment also sets in. And when this happens your ability to fight, or flight is also compromised. Basically, an individual's psychic vitality is compromised to the extent where its connection with the being and the existence of the being is severed. And it is therefore that they freeze. There is also an alteration of the chemical balance in the brain, which is similar to the spreading of dark unwanted clouds. There is an instant loss of hope and any vision of future. All this happens when the psychic vitality is assaulted.

Psychologists and counselors often ask individuals susceptible to panic attacks to carry some earthy element which they can touch and feel. Doing this basically helps an individual ground them by enabling the senses to initiate a process of feeling and becoming aware of the body. i will share with you an incident of my cousin and her anxiety.

Due to the vagaries and pressures of life, a phase came in my cousin's life when extant stress increased and anxiety crept in. She would get anxious especially when driving back from work to home. She would also have two kids in the car with her. If by chance the traffic had slowed down or was at a standstill, she would start getting anxious about what will happen next and how will she be able to get out of this. Once this anxiety would hit her, she then would start experiencing panic attacks, and having panic attacks in the middle of a busy interstate highway in the silicon valley area is dangerous. She sought help to reduce her panic attacks that build up due to the What Now question. We came up with a strategy where every day she, while driving home, would call me. i would speak with her to keep her mentally occupied, and more importantly in touch with her body so that she does not experience disembodiment and frozenness while driving a car. This went on for a while and eventually the defenses of the mind and body grew for her to not feel claustrophobic and boxed-in in slow-moving traffic. Her Psychic Vitality returned. i would argue that her ability to absorb radioactivity increased a tad bit more than the uncertainty that prevailed allowing her to not only survive but also to thrive and flourish.

She is much more mature than i am, she takes care and raises two children excellently, has an incredibly supportive husband, and regardless of all the above in this phase of her life and the given time, her maturity, reasoning, and faith, as i mentioned above, went on a hiatus. Her connection with knowledge was severed in that moment making her helpless.

i want to briefly talk about two more of my cousins, who are victims of the What Now question. Both are unable to sleep at night. They both diligently try to go to bed around 10:30 or 11:00 PM but are invariably awake till five in the morning. They just lay awake in bed and keep trying different strategies to put themselves to sleep. It's not that they are not tired or exhausted. They each have three children and have to run around substantially to make sure that they are well-fed and not tardy. In addition, they also have pets. And one also had a job. Despite the unquestioned need for proper sleep, the What Now anxiety keeps them from sleeping. And it is natural that when you sleep at 5:00 AM, it is really difficult and at times impossible to wake up at a decent time in the morning and function like a person who had slept at 11:00 PM. Their mornings are groggy and dull. As mothers they both are endowed with superpowers that allow them to break their inertia and get their bodies to function. One was anxious about the education and future of her children, and the second one was anxious about a barrage of things that were impacting her including menopause, disharmonious marriage, and a mental health scare. They both have different uncertainties pertaining to What Now, but i see them both suffering and my heart goes to many such who are suffering unbeknownst to me because of their inability to absorb the uncertainty around.

i will share yet another instance of what you might find silly but, in my eyes, is a serious form of What Now uncertainty that is plaguing the youth, especially young girls. One semester, in my creative advertising class, i had this sweetest student. Brilliant, yet not entirely sure of her brilliance, she was also always respectful and cordial. She was also happy and cheery but in a subdued way. During a free-flowing brainstorming session, the class as a whole has long discussions about many deep and shallow things. i encourage unhinged dialogues where the topic can change often with no guard rails of where it goes. One day unexpectedly the conversation, staying true to its unhinged essence, was about how often you discharge stool or, simply put, poop. The initial behavioral enquiry was about the use of cell phone in restrooms. All students were discussing this and were giving out their weekly statistics. Well, it was this student's turn, and she with a coffee in her hand said i don't know if i should share this or not. Other students encouraged her, and she said that she has not pooped in a week. Everyone in the class was taken aback. One of the students said that she should visit the doctor immediately after the class, and others were giving her different advice. But the peculiar thing to me was that most other girls in the class were offering her advice, which was based on first-hand experience of having dealt with this issue or from knowing someone close who had suffered from it. This indicated to me that many in class and in their primary and secondary circles were suffering from this unstability.

Having sensitized myself sufficiently to the issues of impending bowel movement, i saw it all around, and it is in particular very radioactive. In another instance, i was part of a team leading a student trip to Italy, we had a young girl who had not used the bathroom for four days. She was bloated and miserable. In the middle of the night, we had to go find constipation-related medicines for her in a "Pharmacia" (pharmacy) shop in Florence. Since we didn't speak the language, we had to play a game of Dumb Charades with the chemists to explain that there was a lot of incoming but no outgoing. And we needed something to help this suffering person. While it was a lot of fun and games in the Pharmacia shop, the one suffering was miserable.

In yet another instance, i was at a conference in Cartagena, Colombia. i co-presented a research paper on online dating at the conference. Later, i was to travel with a friend further to Medellin and Bogota. Her travel anxiety did not allow her to use the bathroom. She seemed visibly distressed after a few days. Upon politely enquiring, she revealed that although she loves traveling, she hates it because her excretory system shuts down when she is on the go. i eventually did some googling and realized that this happens with many humans while traveling.

i reiterate that constipation is a serious "What Now" issue among young girls. This issue was also highlighted in a Bollywood movie (Piku) in an aesthetically appealing and humorous way. The tagline of the movie was "Piku—Motion se hai Emotion." In English, it meant that without proper bowel motion there is no emotion to be had or enjoyed. Going back to Colombia or Italy, it's a panic situation and when you are in a different setting where people don't understand your language, the anxiety is so high that all your knowledge, maturity, and reasoning takes a hiatus. All of this easily makes one radioactive and explosive.

While traveling to many varied places, there is yet another anxiety i have come across and that is climate anxiety. The What Now question pertaining to the changing climate and its immediate and impending repercussions is increasingly becoming a source of uncertainty. Increasing temperatures, mercurial rains and storms, prolonged winters and summers, rising water levels, and many other unaccounted and unpredictable occurrences are increasing anxieties. Some communities and nations, who are already facing the brunt of changed weather patterns, are already panicking in fright and terror. i already supplied, in the first chapter, the example of how the national capital of Jakarta is being shifted to a newly built city.

The question of What Now freezes you and it can be severely debilitating. Imagine the What Now of a wife who had lost her husband or vice versa. Imagine the What Now of those currently living in conflict zones of the world. i had a brief acquaintance with a girl who lived in Syria. One day as we were talking, i asked her how things at her end are. She said well they are great, and we are all alive and safe, but the government today decided that the price of the bread will be three times more than what it was yesterday. Such a level of uncertainty can throw a great many people off. If you are feeding a family of five with your job that pays fixed income and when there is no guarantee of whether the building where you work will be standing tomorrow or would have been bombed and floored in the night, a steep increase in the price of a staple can make you instantly radioactive.

i will now talk about the ultimate What Now question and that makes the elderly profusely radioactive. The anxiety in the elderly, specifically those who are yet healthy and have become cognizant of the failings of the body, is a terrifying trap. There is no escaping one's body. Where would you run away? There is no other option but to be the witness to the disintegration and deterioration of the body. In the US, i do volunteer work with seniors. i have done programs and workshops for seniors that are affiliated with the Senior Centers in two cities. i do workshops on different topics such as Creativity, Fear, and Decluttering. In candid and open conversations with the elderly, the anxiety of what now is pertaining to their imminent death but not necessarily about their death. It is mostly about when you are certain that you are going to die but are not sure what is going to happen to you after that. The finity of body, and the finity of the identity associated with it, its unacceptance is a terrible source of anxiety. Anxiety is about the future. While future is entirely unknown to everyone, not being able to imagine it is a great source unstability and thereof radioactivity.

What If (Fantasy)

What if is a question that generally takes an individual in the realm of fantasy. While fantasy can be filled with pleasure or even be soothing, reality in its comparison is not. The journey from reality to fantasy is often an outcome of the What If question.

The What If question comfortably transports an individual in the realm of fantasy and our brains also support and encourage these rides. What i wonder though is that in the moments that you or i or anyone for that matter is in the realm of fantasy, do they also exist in reality? As in do they do their chores? Can they pay sufficient attention? Can they properly function in the real world while they are exploring and engaged in the fantasy world?

What do you think, can a person exist in both the planes and states of existence? Ask around and do an informal survey of people around you and see what they have to say. You will get a feel of what people think around you aside from what this book has to offer.

At the core we are all creative beings. Humanity has consistently strived to and succeeded greatly in transforming its fantasies to reality. To fantasize and transform that fantasy into a reality has been our way of progressing and evolving. Our ability to keep pondering and manifesting alternatives is inexhaustible. Fantasy, hope, and grit have made things possible. However, in the major shuffle, those who ended up being powerful allowed their greed to rid the masses of their ability to fantasize, be hopeful, and remain gritty. The creators and setters of system have created systems where many are living to fulfill the fantasies of a few. The grit to strive and bring fantasy to life has been systematically attacked. What has been actually tabooed and stigmatized is the plurality of fantasies. This has been done by labeling such a plurality as chaos, anarchy, or lawlessness. On the one hand, fantasy has been curbed consistently, and on the other hand, it is also a source of radioactivity when remains unfulfilled. This makes it a double-edged sword.

One of my fantasies is to have a large home with one common dining area. All my family and extended family members would also be living here. We all live together. As a child for the longest time my fantasy revolved around togetherness. That people are happier when they are together with their loved ones. Hence, in my fantasy land, i had designed this architectural marvel where everyone would come together to eat and spend time but then would also have their private living areas and residences under the same roof. i never expressed this fantasy of mine to anyone to avoid being embarrassed. But now that i have grown (inarguably) and you could even say matured to some degree (some would vehemently argue), i realize that this fantasy will never work out in my lifetime because such a fantasy requires sacrifice on everyone's part. And everyone is not always willing to sacrifice. Moreover, i am yet to possess the material and emotional means necessary for transforming my fantasy into reality.

The What If fantasies have a peculiar trait to them. When we fantasize such things there is somehow, ingrained in the process, an elimination of the notion of discomfort. A majority of our fantasies, if you come to think of it, have no discomfort. There is tremendous comfort in them. Any labor, difficulty, toil, and effort magically disappear whereas that is not the case in reality. Reality is abundantly filled with difficulty and discomfort.

Thus far i have discussed about the fantasies that one would want to transform into reality. When one is not able to do so s/he could become sad and feel dejected. But there is a whole other side of the coin here. What about the fantasies that one does not want to transform into reality? This What If is the more potent source of instability for an individual. The What If questions such as What If i Fail or What If she says no are the debilitating ones. The negative or the unwanted side of fantasies is a dark side filled with paralyzing potency.

For a moment think of your fantasies. What are the areas in which the What If question presents to you? Make a list of your fantasies in the space given below. For the moment restrict your fantasies to not more than five.

List your Fantasies

1 ______________________________

2 ______________________________

3 ______________________________

4 ______________________________

5 ______________________________

Reflect based on the fantasies you have listed as to what do your fantasies teach you about yourself. Think if you have the ability to alter your fantasies. What emotions do your fantasies bring to you? Are they positive or negative?

The world of What If is a magical world because you can feel so many things without actually experiencing them in reality. You can feel pain, joy, happiness, tension, stress, and what not. You can feel everything. The goal is to use fantasies to our advantage and not to our disadvantage. Many times, it is not in our control how they get used but our constant endeavor should be to use them to our advantage.

Why Not (Injustice)

Why not is the childish temper tantrum that prevails within the human cognitive system. This sense of injustice emerges as a result of ignorance, or absence of wisdom to accept a given outcome. Ignorance about the reasons for something to not have happened sparks the dark thoughts of injustice. Thoughts of injustice being done to oneself typically attack objectivity and an immediate suspension of objectivity takes place. This is often followed by the suspension of wisdom, logic, and reason. When ignorance prevails about the precise cause for a particular effect, then the primary thing that surfaces as an explanation is injustice. And once it surfaces then the locus of fault instantly shifts from the individual to the many unexplained and unknown vagaries and eccentricities of the world.

Including time in this mess business of injustice can extend the severity of the consequence of this line of inquiry by making it about why not until now. Impatience can make every moment of why not until now bitter and increasing unstability. It is very easy for such bitterness to transform into radioactivity. Lack of acceptance comes from the place of ego. Undue centrality of the self can also bring in unacceptability. Ego, ignorance, and sense of injustice when they form the clouds, they most certainly hide any and every ability of an individual to be discerning.

i was in my 9th standard in the year 1999. We used to have two major exams before our year's final exam. In my first exam, i received 14 marks out of 40. i had barely passed. It's called getting passing marks. i was good at Math, i always performed well in it. But as soon as the 9th standard started something happened and my performance in Math went drastically down. It did come as a surprise to me because i had never gotten passing marks before. Well, i did not pay much heed to it and carried on without asking for help. i just couldn't understand how much the subject of Math had changed in less than a year. i was good at numbers, and i still am good with them. But now i was not dealing with numbers as much. i was mostly dealing with the letters of alphabet. Mostly the letters X, Y, Z, A, B, and C. My brain could not make sense of the alphabet-driven math. Well, in the second major exam, i failed.

i had never failed before, so i never had to worry about so many things that i had heard from others. But when i failed i realized that it was not as bad as people made it to be. It is nothing but an added opportunity to relearn. And the stigma attached to it is also an illusion. Maybe because i had not failed before or i did not have a history of failing, people behaved differently with me in my failure. Also, unfortunately, we are not properly taught and trained to process failure. Failure is a part of our existence. Failure, as i come to think of it, is something that you cannot reconcile and be at peace with. Failure always has to be aggressively dealt with and eradicated from one's life.

Conclusion

These three questions, i know for a fact, lurk somewhere in my conscience ready to resist it as it yearns for stability. The nature of these three questions is quite bewildering. These questions have the potential of creating jumbles in a straight-thinking line. As i ponder about these three questions, i have surmised that they are the real Pandora's box. Come to think of it, once opened there is no counting or imagination of the things that come out of this box.

While each of the above questions can create a whirlwind of unstable radiation buildup in the mind body and life of an individual it is extremely vital to bear in mind that these very damaging questions can also be launch pads for radioactive flourishing when dealt with maturity and wisdom. The very same boat that can drown us in the middle of a water body also has the potential to carry us far beyond safely over the deepest water body. What if, why not, and what now can present opportunities to radioactively flourish by growing, learning, and comprehending one's own follies and either biased working of the brain. Our brain does nothing other than create illusions and mirages for us to remain indulgent in everything else but reality.

This is probably why renowned and revered Indian ascetic Adi Shankaracharya said "Jagat Mithya, Brahma Satya." In the process of radioactive flourishing our brain, which is the moderator, moderates the jagat and presents it to us in a narrow and transient fashion. This ephemerality of the world as we see, and experience is nothing but a little here and there of the balance like a few chemicals in the brain. Deeper clarity, objectivity, emotional maturity, and intellectual maturity are critical to reverse or pause or nullify the onslaught of the greed-led and brain-fed radioactivity. The role of wisdom and conscience is to cut across on sensory stimulators that propel radioactivity and just directly get to the radioactive flourishing by making things clear and life simple.

6

WHAT ANGERS YOU CONTROLS YOU

Anger is a corrosive force that throngs in humankind. This corrosive force is not just damaging to us but also to the people around us. Anger not only uproots us from our evolutionary grounding and progress of 10,000 years but also consumes our proclivities and actions. Globally, individual anger and an individual's angry explosions are on the rise. Especially, the illusion or imagined reality-led intolerant version of anger is particularly dangerous. These explosions, although are, from one perspective, a normal and natural way of securing stability, bring with them unprecedented divisiveness. Unity of culture and the cultural ethos of togetherness are jeopardized as a result of angry explosions. Expression of anger is a sign that the radioactivity is not absorbed as much as it should. This chapter will look at anger in depth and will problematize the natural or rather intuitive way of reducing instability. It does so because it is critical to comprehend that "what angers you controls you."

M&M

Anger is the most common and go-to response to instability. This is because, once a human becomes radioactive, anger is the quickest way to release instability. Behavioral explosions originating from anger are therefore very common.

A garden can have many different varieties of flowers. Just as gardens, humans too have an array of reactions and responses to different situations and circumstances. Anger is an emotion that should find no place in our garden. As soon as anger finds a place in our garden, it starts destroying everything around it. Modern psychology understands and looks at anger as an emotional response. Modern psychology proposes M&M as a way to deal with anger issues.

DOI: 10.4324/9781032627564-6

M&M refers to managing anger and making amends. Managing anger is a big business and people pay a lot of money for it. Making amends is about approaching the person or the group toward which one has shown aggression and asking for forgiveness. M&M methodology, while effective, is very much like a hamster in a wheel in the long run. Lot of running but no movement. Understanding anger and its roots is very critical for a long-term intervention. Hence, eliminating the root cause of anger is needed more than the management of it and making amends after it.

i came across a powerful story about anger, which i want to share with you. Long ago, there was a boy who had a reputation for getting angry. At the drop of a hat, he would get angry and become uncontrollable. This often landed him in trouble. Due to his inability to control his temper, he was also an easy target for manipulation. One day, the boy got really mad and did something that crossed every threshold. His parents were displeased and deeply concerned for his wellbeing. They were also worried about how they could help their child to navigate this world if anger was the only reaction he had to everything around him. So, the parents thought long and hard that night. They came up with a strategy and decided to act on it.

The next day, when the boy, got angry, as usual, the father stepped in and said, "Dear son, take this bag of nails. It has a bunch of different nails. My dear son, I want you to do this one thing for me." The son looked ragingly at his father and curtly said, "What? What do you want me to do?" The father handed him a bag of nails and proceeds to say, "Every time you get angry, I want you to take this bag and nail one nail with this hammer in our fence. Can you please do that much for us?" Begrudgingly and angrily, the boy said yes.

Next day, the boy went and hammered a bunch of nails at different times when he was angry. At the end of the day, when the father counted the nails, there were some 40–50 of them. This meant that the boy got angry 40–50 times that day. This exercise went on for a few weeks. After a while, the boy started seeing something in himself and started controlling his anger. When the father went and checked after a month, there were only 20 new nails. There was a reduction. The father was happy with the progress. Over time, the boy realized that it was easy to control his temper and not lose it, instead of hammering a nail, and ruining the fence.

One fine day, the boy went to the father and jubilantly said, "Father, today I have not had to hammer a single nail in the fence. Does it mean that my task here is over?"

The father said, "Not yet." This irked the boy, but he controlled himself. The father continued, "I want you to do something else."

Frustrated, the boy said, "What? What now? I have done everything that you told me. What now?"

The father calmly said, “Every day when you are able to control yourself, I want you to go and pull out one nail from the fence.” The boy was bewildered again. “What new weird stuff is this?”

Ultimately, he yielded and said, “Okay.”

The next day, he went in the evening to pull out a nail. It was difficult, but he somehow managed. He did the same thing the next day. He could not do it the day after because he was unable to control himself, so he had to hammer a nail instead of removing it. This went on for months, and he would have so much difficulty and trouble to remove nails during that time.

Finally, there came a day when he removed the last nail from the fence. Upon removing the nail, he went to his father and said, “I have something to tell you.” The father enquired, “Yes, what is it?” The boy said, “I have pulled out every nail from the fence.”

The father said, “You know what that means.” The boy said, “Yes, I do.” The father said, “You have done very well. Now, let us go and take a look at the fence.” They both walked out and from a distance looked at the fence. Observing the fence brought an instant sadness to the boy’s face. The father calmly said,

> The fence will never be the same. Take a look at the fence. When you say or do things in anger, they always leave a scar or a mark. Just like this fence. Look at all the holes and the marks on it, even after you made amends. Every time something is done in anger, it destroys a part of you and the world around you that can never be undone.

Poke a Hole

Based on the story let us do a little exercise. Take an A4 size paper and hang it on your office desk or a place where you can see it and access it. Every time you become angry and lash out angrily, poke a hole in it. Every time you are unable to control yourself and lash out at someone or your own self, go ahead and poke a hole in it. Observe the page after one week.

Take another sheet of paper and do the same for another week. Repeat this for a month with four papers.

After a month sit with the paper and analyze the holes in the pages. What do they mean to you? What do they mean to others around you? How does it alter the environment around you? How does it change the behavior of people around you toward you? (this you will not realize easily. You must persevere to discover this. But people do behave differently in the presence of anger).

Anger and Radioactivity

Angry explosion is contrary to radioactive flourishing. Upon becoming radioactive, when a person loses control and explodes, s/he is not flourishing. S/he does so to reduce his or her own instability, but the means adopted is, as stated earlier, corrosive. It creates negativity around the person where others don't appreciate him or her internally. The reason behind the unappreciativeness is because an angry person adds to the instability of others around, and it is not preferable to add to instability rather than getting rid of it. Once an individual is uncontrollable s/he loses the ability to focus the explosive energy.

As a child i would ask my family and relatives to tell me about our family folks who preceded us. Thematically, stories of my forefathers revolved primarily around their anger. i am certain they had other emotions too but all they are now remembered for was their anger. This was disappointing for me because that's not how i want to be known and remembered. Growing up, i was a fun-loving and happy child, but my bouts of anger were also an equally dominant part of my persona. Something i was clearly never proud of. i have fought with anger a lot. i was handed my bag of nails and i have hammered so many of them to the fence and removed them. And regretfully my fence is never going to be the same as it was earlier. Thankfully, my urge to be in control of my senses and life overpowered my anger and prevented the fence from being ruined further.

While in school, i remember that a teacher asked me to stand up and read aloud the chapter of the day. This was a common practice. Teachers would typically choose students who could project their voice and had clear pronunciations. And since i could do that, i was typically picked for the task. A student who was sitting behind me was trying to distract me so that i would make a mistake and get yelled at by the teacher. i was not getting much distracted with his silly distracting gimmicks. However, there was something within me that wanted to show him that i am superior to him, and that i had power over him. For a while, i did not do anything. i was able to control myself despite his silly gimmicks. i was absorbing the radioactivity despite the urge. But at one point i felt a sharp prick in my back.

That student had taken out his compass and pricked me with the sharp metallic end of it. i vividly remember this moment because this is when i lost control. The instability in me became radioactive so fast that i failed entirely in absorbing it. And as a result, i exploded. i turned around, stared in his eyes for a moment. i saw in his eyes that he knew he was in the wrong and was apologetic too. i wish i had controlled myself because he had already realized that he had done something that had crossed a boundary. i let loose a tight slap on his right cheek in front of the class. The teacher looked at us with a puzzled look. i escaped my teacher's punishment or repercussion because my explosion was a reaction and not an instigation. But i cannot escape my heavy conscience till this day which keeps reminding me that i was unable to control my radioactive explosion.

Perhaps i could have controlled myself if i had really tried hard and especially not succumbed to my ego. i share this incident here because ego, which is within us, plays a prominent role in angry explosions. An instigation may not always be of a magnitude that requires a severe anger-ridden backlash. But once it makes home inside us, ego starts fueling the fire. Unchecked ego makes the littlest of an instigation bigger that it really is, and an individual ends up making him or herself more and more unstable. The spark may have come from the outside, but the fire is being kept alive and aggravated internally.

Another instance where i was controlled by anger was in May of 2023. And it was the one person with whom my smaller explosions unfortunately happened often, my mother. While growing up i have relished the food lovingly cooked and prepared by her. i got accustomed to that taste. But as time went by, three things happened. We had an addition to our family, my sister. With progressing age my father developed cholesterol and high blood pressure, and my mother wanted to keep a check on her weight. My sister when she was young could not tolerate spicy food. My father reduced his intake of salt substantially. And my mother cut back on adding sugar in the food to keep a watch on her sugar intake. Amidst all this, i suddenly stopped getting the tasty food that i was always getting. No chili, no salt, and no sugar. Well, let me change no to low chili, low salt, and low sugar.

For the longest time, i kept saying to my mother that there is something off about the food that you make but i did not have the knowledge about the ingredients that were missing. i instinctively, through the sense of vision first, smell second, and taste third would keep feeling that something was off. But what was that something, i did not know. i needed it all. i was a teenager, who was the captain of a sports team and would physically exert for six hours every day in temperatures of 100° F (or 40° C) and more. Well, i needed calories, but i also wanted the taste that used to be a companion to the calories. This created tiffs and arguments between my mother and i when we would all have our meals together.

i also recall instances where my instability became so high that anger would control me, and i would leave the dining table in the middle of the meal or just not eat. Upon deeper reflection, i realized that the deeper source of my instability was not always from the tasteless food. Sometimes, yes. But not always. The deeper source was the lack of acknowledgement or the challenge to the means through which i perceived the world and gained knowledge. When i would say that something was different in the food, the response would be that we find it well balanced, you are the one who always needs everything extra. The narrative in my family as well as my extended family that prevails to this day is that Arpan likes more sugar in his food. i have tried to repair that narrative a thousand times that, no, i do not like extra sugar, but i just prefer balanced food, how it used to be.

My efforts over the past 15 years have not dented the age-old narrative even a bit. Nonetheless, the argument that everything is fine you only need things extra challenged my system of perceiving and knowing the world that was serving me so well in the world in a twisted way at the dining table. That argument was indirectly disrespecting and undermining the conclusions that i was deriving. And i was not able to, deep down, reconcile that how could something that works everywhere fail at the dining table. This lack of reconciliation, along with the ego and pride that my system was a superiorly functioning system, and not getting the desired taste at the time when one is hungry took my unstability to the levels where it became immensely radioactive. i most definitely then did not have the needed ability to absorb it, so would sadly and foolishly end up exploding.

i have worked so much on myself and now i can absorb most of the dining table conundrum but then there are occasions when i am unable to absorb my radioactivity fully. i remember one instance a couple of years ago where there was a mismatch between the taste my neural networks remembered and what was served on the table, and this just instantly made me radioactive. After years of working on myself i was able to absorb the radioactivity sufficiently which in turn prevented me from angrily exploding. But i still had to excuse myself from the table and be away for fifteen minutes before joining everyone back. At that moment, i just could not process what was going on in me. My mindfulness was compromised substantially. This is one aspect of my life which has destabilized me the most. Thankfully it is a very small aspect and not something dire.

Ego and Expectations play a critical role in destabilizing humans. Humans expect a lot. Humans expect too much from other people. Humans expect much from their lives and situations. What happens when these expectations are not met? Some or the other form of unstability in the form of disappointment and subsequent anger, which explodes like a volcano. What are some of the things that you expect from others? You must take some time to reflect on how your unmet expectations cause you to be angry. Given below is a table with three columns. Use the first column to write down the unmet expectations that you have from yourself or people around you or the world or a given situation. In the second column corresponding to your unmet expectation, write the way in which it destabilized you and how did you explode as a result of it. In the third column you should note down the people impacted by it. Here in this column, you can also list down yourself because some people focus their anger on their own self and hurt themselves. i have written down one from my life that may serve as an example for you to continue (Table 6.1).

TABLE 6.1 Anger Activity

Unmet Expectation	*Nature of Angry Explosion*	*People impacted by it*
Food with the right balance of chili, salt, sugar, and tamarind	Leave the dinner table, say mean things, not eat at all, display disgruntlement	My mother, me, my father, and my sister

Anger is one of the emotional reactions that humans have in their quiver. This is not the only arrow we have. But sadly, this is the one arrow that we quickly mount on the bow and shoot. Anger is mostly a reaction and seldom a response. Here it is important to learn the distinction between a reaction and a response. When we are reacting, we are not really taking time to process. We are not engaging our cognitive faculties, we are not engaging our mental faculties. We do not even consult with our inner voice, which is the voice of our conscience. We just react. And anger is fired. It doesn't come back. The fence will never be the same. The A4 size of paper will never be the same. Our friends, when they do something contrary to our expectations, we say things to them in anger and it always leaves scars.

Something else that one needs to think about or consider is that in the Northern part of India there are many rivers that emerge from the Himalayas. Most of those rivers are life-giving. They provide an entire ecosystem with nourishment. And there are some rivers that are uncontrollable and bring nothing but destruction. Over the years people, individuals, societies, and governments have tried to manage these rivers. No matter how much they try to manage these rivers or make amends, the river still brings destruction. All the rivers are very similar to the wide array of emotional responses that we have at our disposal. Some like laughing it off, neglecting, thinking about it and pausing for a while, etc. are like the life-giving rivers that nourish the human ecosystem and help it in flourishing it. Whereas anger is like that one river which always brings destruction, no matter how much we try. Anger is something that we want to actively move away from. Basically, move way from reacting to responding.

Response is a well-processed and well-equipped approach to a situation. Imagine that in your vicinity there is a little fire. You see the smoke and you realize that your neighbor's house is on fire. You immediately dash to help. But you don't have the ability or the qualification to douse the fire because you cannot evaluate and conclude correctly what caused the fire. Well even if you can by chance detect it, but still without properly understanding the nature of fire you may use the wrong method to douse the fire. This can in turn cause more damage not just to the property, but you also put yourself in harm's way. This is what a reaction means, whereas the fire department comes in a certain type of uniform that protects them from fire. They come equipped with knowledge about the different types of fire and what material is best to diffuse it and douse it. They come prepared and that is why they are known as first responders and not first reactors. Similarly in situations where an individual does not act or behave in a way that you expected, first one must assess that does this need a reaction or a response. Would i say the same things if i were responding as opposed to the time when i was reacting? This distinction is very important, and i would suggest the reader to keep in mind.

Three things to remember and keep in mind from this chapter are the following:

- The fence will never be the same.
- Some flowers that have no scent should not be in our garden.
- The distinction between reaction and response. Anger is typically a reaction and seldom a response.

Anger is the biggest deterrent that suspends our ability to process and make meaning. Anger makes you delusional because you are not in your control. Something else is in control of you. Whatever makes you angry controls you.

Anger is typically associated with frustration of not being able to fulfill desires. Many desires pertaining to power, prestige, partner, money, and more are in play. When one is unable to fulfill a desire that one is after profusely, our mind is disturbed. We start becoming more and more unstable and eventually radioactive. Unfulfilled desires just like unmet expectations are dangerous. Desired are also not static. They keep changing. Based on the age and stage of life that you are in, your desires will also keep changing. When i was in my 3rd standard, i expressed a desire to have an eraser that my friend possessed. It was a fancy eraser that was bought from the US. When i was doing my business administration, i desired for a corporate job with a role that would come with many perks such as the special treatment when you travel business class and the comfort that comes with it. i also desired something from the relationships i had with my parents. One of the desires and expectations i had was regarding food, which i have already mentioned earlier. This unfulfilled desire changed the nature of my relationship with them. It made the relation a bit sour. i felt like they were all being selfish and catered to their needs while comfortably compromising my desires. There can be many more desires that can play a role. Many younger siblings desire for new clothes but they are often given the previously worn ones. All these are sources of frustration. And much of it stays in check where a person is able to overcome it easily but sometimes it is uncontrollable.

Ages and stages make a big difference. Many folks are now unhappy and frustrated with politics and news. News has pervaded people's lives way more than it could previously. Also, the frustration with politicians and their shenanigans and misgivings is frustrating. i have encountered many folks around me being enraged and mad about it. A very dear friend of mine who has played a foundational role at a given stage in my life simply cannot control himself. When we friends hang out after a day's work people have started to actively avoid him because he gets angry and says things that are unpleasant or irksome. He reads a lot and is well informed so what he says even makes sense but not everyone wants to be that informed or alert and share the same opinion with him. But he expects that everyone should live and think by a certain code, and everyone is disappointing, and he gets mad and yells at them. All he expects is for people to vote with proper knowledge and understanding. But it is a vicious radioactive cycle where both parties keep feeding off of one another's radioactivity. The politically charged climate does not help anyone.

Another thing that created polarization was the coronavirus pandemic where we were all forced to live in enclosed spaces. We were not allowed to go out. Abandon our lives as they were. Many were also going through immense financial pressures. The distended proximity to so many members of the family was frustrating for so many. In a country like India where homes are small, and the number of people is many, forced cohabitation and subsequent interactions can make people radioactive rapidly. My colleague and fellow researcher who studies and does work in domestic violence and trauma informed me that the instances of domestic violence increased manyfold during the pandemic. Radioactive explosions between partners became violent and in many places in the US, shelters were filled to capacity during the pandemic.

It is important for us to understand that when our desires are not fulfilled, our mind becomes disturbed. Funnily, where do our desires emerge from? Our mind. When we spend way too much time thinking and fixating about one thing for example in my case the food that i was served, this is when you develop attachment toward it. i had an attachment to the food of a certain taste and flavor. When attachment develops, it slowly transforms into a keen desire. A desire is a two-way sword explains the *Bhagwat Gita*. It cuts inside and outside. Desire is never eliminated by fulfilling it. If you satisfy your desire, all it leads toward is greed. If you desire something and if you fulfill your desire by obtaining that something, the desire does not go. Satisfying one's desire will not lead to satiating it, it will only lead to greed. It will leave you wanting more. Most people i come across are in the need for wanting and accumulating more and more. Seldom, and that too if you are incredibly lucky, you come across someone who genuinely does not want more. This is the first edge of desire that it does not get satiated by fulfilling it.

The second edge of desire is that if you do not fulfill it, then it leads to frustration and eventual anger. So, fulfilling desire on the one hand and on the other hand not fulfilling your desire or being obstructed from fulfilling your desire and feeling helpless can also lead to anger. And we must understand the nature of this double-edged sword because without the clarity, it will control you. Bear in mind that anger is a reaction. It is not an entity by itself. It arises when you feel helpless, or when there is an obstruction in fulfilling your desire, or there are attachments and as soon as anger or its twin greed comes into play the ability to process information rationally and with sanity disappears.

It is one thing to be angry and it is another to become anger. There are people who get angry and that sort of defines their life path and decisions and behaviors. They are the ones that are unable to absorb radioactivity and hence explode. To be angry can happen in an instant and can dissipate. But then becoming angry ourselves is dangerous. To become synonymous with anger is unfortunate. There is a subtle difference between being angry and becoming angry.

Empty Boat

Let me share here the story of the empty boat. This story will help you think about anger. Imagine that you are in the middle of a big lake. You are rowing your boat and minding your business. Everything is calm and serene. Everything is idyllic. But then suddenly you spot that there is another boat. When you look closely you realize that it is empty. After a while you realize that this empty boat is coming toward you. You become curious about why is this boat coming toward you. You get on with your life and you try to neglect but it comes precariously close to your boat. Ultimately it comes and collides with your boat. Shaking everything. Creating a lot of ripples around where it destroys everything calm and serene around you.

> What do you do?
> An empty boat has come out of nowhere and collided with you.
> What do you do?
> Who would you end up being angry at?
> Write whoever comes to your mind in the space below.

1 ____

2 ____

3 ____

Most people in this sort of a thought experiment are upset and angry with their own luck, and some are mad about the wind or the water current, and some about this unknown person who let this boat loose in the water. People emote first because their idyllic setting is disturbed. People don't naturally investigate because their calm is lost. However, it may likely be possible to change how we experience and act out the emotion of anger based on how we think.

So, let's think about this particular instance of the boat and see what changes within us when we think of it differently. And there are lots of ways to think about it.

One way to think is how would my emotion and reaction be different if there was someone in the boat.

____
____
____

Consequently, what if there was an animal in the boat? A cute puppy. What if a ferocious-looking hound was in the boat?

____
____
____

What if a frail old man who resembles your grandfather was in the boat/ what if a young man was in the boat? What if an adult was in the boat? How would all these change your response?

____
____
____

Just like a boat in water, our very moving existence creates a wake. Faster waves, which have longer wave lengths, leave behind wider wakes. And slower waves, which have short wave lengths, leave behind narrower wakes. Depending on who we are and what is our individual wavelength we are anyways leaving a wake in our trail. This is something that we have very little to no control over. So, when another boat collides with our boat, ripples are created. My challenge to us is that regardless of the fact that the boat was empty or not, and who was in it, what can we do to ensure that there are little to no ripples? Can we start focusing on that direction at least. Let me give you a related example of action taken in that direction where also the symbolic boat is not empty. It has a very specific and certain type of population.

Imagine a situation when you go to a restaurant with your friends or family. You most certainly expect that the food that is delivered to you is the food that you ordered. What would you do if you ordered Indian curry and instead got Italian pasta, and your friend ordered Chinese noodles and instead got Mediterranean hummus?

Say if you were a group of 10 and only 3 of you got what you ordered, and the rest were served something they had not ordered. This form of unmet expectation would most certainly make a patron instantly radioactive and instead of absorbing it, s/he would deal this heavy-handedly with abundant anger mixed with words of humiliation pertaining to incompetence and inability to provide proper service. This is like the empty boat coming out of nowhere and colliding with you.

Waiting at restaurants if you carefully think about it is not easy. i say this because it requires a server to remember a wide variety of things for a short amount of time for a lot of different sets of people, and the expectation is to get it right every time. Servers, all over the world, are expected to not succumb to the common human follies of selective listening, selective interpretation, and selection transmission. Servers, all over the world, do this average human behavior-defying stunt every day.

Shiro Oguni saw this thing in an entirely different way. When i say different, it means creative and compassionate. He started to think along the lines of what can be done to not create ripples when the collision happens. So, he opened a restaurant in Japan called The Restaurant of Mistaken Orders, where all the servers are elderly and suffering from dementia. The patrons are made well aware of this fact about the servers. Servers greet the patrons and take their orders but when they serve the food most likely it is not what the patron ordered. These elderly individuals who have served society for such a long time in different capacities and abilities, now cannot remember, and for no fault of their own.

Shiro had visited an old age home for the elderly with dementia and their isolation saddened him. This sadness is also a form of unstability. But he also felt that there is no need for these individuals to remain isolated and there must be a way to make them a part of society. Once integrated in the work of The Restaurant of Mistaken Orders such elderly folks found a place in the society. Moreover, the cause, the compassion, and the creative framing ensured that although 35% times the orders are wrong and despite this high inaccuracy, the satisfaction of dining at this restaurant is measured at quite high 99% of the time.

The empty boat is one of my favorite reflective thought experiments because it allows me to identify and study my self-centeredness, my biases, my beliefs, my kindness, my compassion, and my fondness/love/obsession for my space. If extended well it also gives a sneak peek into my displaced aggression-related tendencies.

Displaced Aggression and Locus of Control

In my research on green marketing, our research team was interested in examining the role of Locus of Control (LOC) in green purchase decision-making. Locus of Control as a variable and a concept has stayed with me since. i like Locus of Control because it is a manipulable variable. With intervention, especially information and knowledge based, LOC can be manipulated. Most of the self-help books and coaches on the planet do pretty much the same as the above. They work with their clients and alter in the understanding of the client that LOC is much more internal and, in their charge, as opposed to external. There are two types of LOC: Internal and External. When a person feels that they have no control over the outcome of a situation or any occurrence within a situation and that the entire control lies in the hands of an entity other than them then that person is said to feel and believe to be suffering from external LOC. Many people often feel that during elections. They feel that their one vote will not matter amidst the hundreds of millions of other votes and that they have no control over the outcome. This feeling of external LOC is also a source of instability and resulting radioactivity.

As opposed to External LOC, in the Internal LOC, a person feels and believes that they have control over the outcome. Internal LOC is not a potent source of instability and subsequent radioactivity because the person feels in control and in charge. When the locus of control is external, there is another concept called displaced aggression that comes into play. Displaced aggression is a form of radioactive fallout but a delayed one. Instead of an instant radioactive reaction, in displaced aggression, a person holds on to their aggression deep in them for a long time waiting for an opportune moment to unleash the aggression.

Displaced aggression is more damaging in my opinion from the perspective of radioactivity. I say so because an individual stays radioactive and in an unstable state for a really long time. And all this time they have to pretend as if they are normal and not really bothered. And while they do so they keep planning and plotting and scheming about how and when to get their revenge. Many acts of violent extremism are examples of displaced aggression. The trigger event for such instances would have occurred years if not decades ago. People wait for their time and then strike when the opposite party is the most vulnerable. This staggered version of instability often leads to unbelievably problematic and fatal outcomes. There is another angle to displaced aggression that one should also not forget to look at or consider. Person A may have caused agony to person B and person B takes it out on an entirely different set of individuals, which creates a chain of anger, suppression, discrimination, and lashing out. The powerful takes it out on the powerless.

One needs to be extra mindful about if displaced aggression is working through them or if the different locus of control makes them angry and unstable. There is a lot more to say about these two, but I do not want to make this chapter about them both. So, I conclude this portion by saying that Locus of Control and Displaced Aggression are two forces that one needs to keep in mind while understanding anger because regardless of whether you feel that you have an internal locus of control or you don't have any control and the locus of control is external to you, ultimately your anger will control you. I want to now introduce you to something I find is of much more significance for you as you move away from this chapter. It is the Hole of Anger.

Hole of Anger

As a hypothesis, it is fair to say that what angers you controls you. This makes it important to map out and rat out the things that anger you. i have prepared for you an illustration of a Hole of Anger. This circular figure should help you to identify the things that anger you and subsequently control you. In my experience when i completed the Hole of Anger, i realized that anywhere between 80% and 90% of the things that anger me are minor or trivial things. With very little effort one can take control over the controllers.

The Hole of Anger is divided into three major areas: family, personal, profession. There are agents of anger in the family that behave and act to irate you. These are the individuals that are consuming your energy, emotion, and time. Personal frontier includes one's own insufficiencies, insecurities, fears, habits, health situation, and friends. This is something you can seldom get rid of because it is very difficult to get rid of one's body and mind. i have included friends in this category because friends are a personal choice. They appear in our lives and disappear from them on our choice and desire. On the professional front there are two broad choices including job and education. Job here symbolically stands for any and every kind of work situation. It could be a 9–5 job or even your business, or a startup. All your endeavors are conducted with the intention of earning money and in the process giving back some value to the society.

There can be many more areas that can get you angry and you feel free to add to your hole of anger. However, these three will cover a large majority of your causes for anger. Use the below template to map out and identify your controllers. The Hole of Anger is a good reflective exercise and a subsequent reminder that will enable you to identify when a controller is around and is actively or passively trying to weaken you. What are the behaviors you exhibit when you are angry is also a critical area of comprehension. But at this stage, i will restrict the scope of this to identifying the triggers and stimulators of anger in you and mapping them accurately.

Take a photocopy of this photo or scan it and then print it out on a larger A3 size paper. Map out things and identify the triggers that push you constantly towards the Hole of Anger. This reflective exercise will help you in identifying areas that you can work on to eschew controlling anger. One thing that will help you reconcile and subside your anger is a very important line with which i want to end this chapter. This quote is also otherwise important for Radioactive Flourishing in general. This quote from Rajmohan Gandhi does justice to the flourishing portion of the book.

> "When people who really have every right to be angry forgive, that is when the chain of hatred is broken."

This is radioactive flourishing summarized in one line. i will repeat this again in the book for the simple purposes and hopes of you remembering it (Figure 6.1).

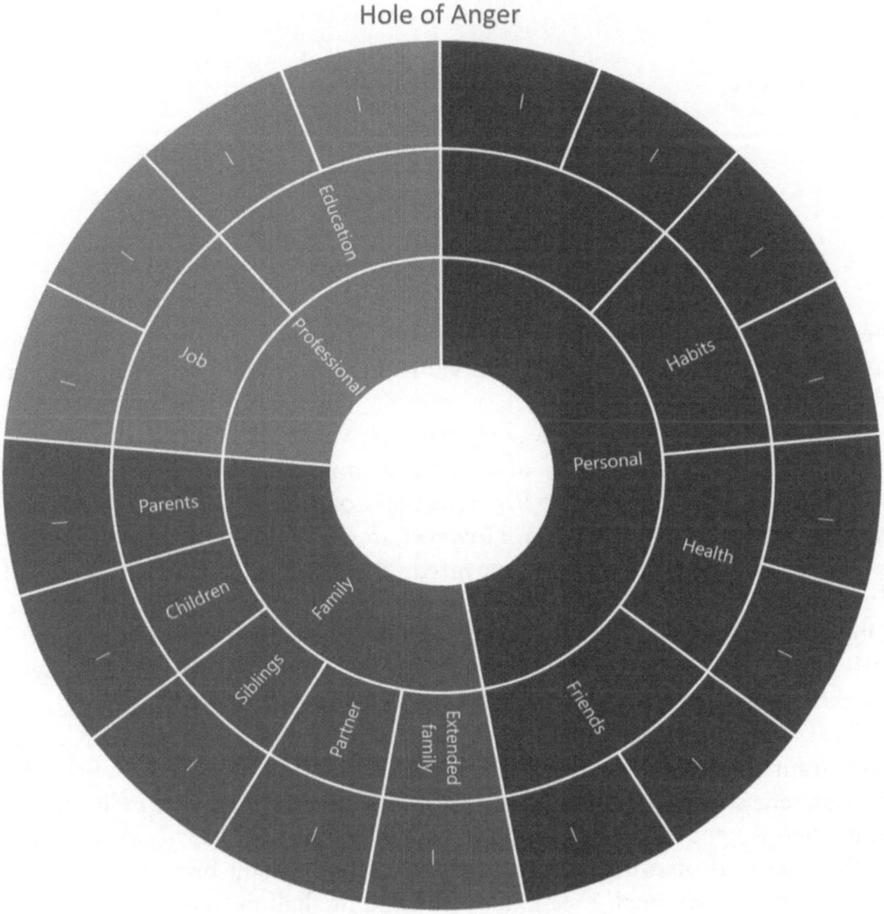

FIGURE 6.1 Hole of Anger.

7

FEAR

Fear is a *Bhrama*, an illusion. While it exists, it actually does not exist. For as long as it exists it destabilizes an individual and moves him or her away from their stable state.

Kartik was my friend. He was a great guy. We studied in college together. He was one of those guys who always had a smile on his face. We all saw the same smile on his face for the first two years of college and even in the first half of the third year of college. However, in the final leg of the college that smile faded and eventually disappeared. For some of us in my group of friends, it was quite shocking, pretty much like the sun had stopped shining. Obviously, we inquired but did not get any response from him. With his most striking feature eclipsed, his presence became depressing for the otherwise cheerful group, and slowly he disappeared into the shadows.

Years later, I ran into him, and we went together for a meal in the Khichdi restaurant. That's where I flourish, in the Khichdi restaurant, which provides 40 different styles of khichdi. Anyhow, we were talking about many things and when we got to the desert, I quietly asked him what was bothering him in the final year of college. He realized that I had caught him off guard, but he gave in since so much time had passed and life had moved on. Kartik told me that he had a fear of facing interviews. His fear was so extreme that he just could not smile.

All our campus placement-related interviews were conducted in the final year of the college and Kartik has a stellar resume. On the basis of his stellar resume, he got selected for several interviews but due to his fear, he never made it past the interview round. The fear of having to face another interview, he said, was so daunting that he just couldn't be in a stable state anymore. He could not smile, he could not interact well and started remaining

DOI: 10.4324/9781032627564-7

more and more subdued and aloof. We were all a witness to this transition, I told him, and hence we inquired. He nodded and said that he was so embarrassed that he chose not to say anything. Those three months were the worst of his life. There was so much instability in him that he became radioactive. His radiation emitted differently where he became estranged from his own friends and had to endure loneliness.

This may sound paradoxical but fear, although an illusion, is very real. It is at the very least very real to the person experiencing it. And everyone suffers from one or the other kind of fear. The kingdom of fear touches the lives of practically every living entity on the planet. Even animals and birds are live in fear of being predated upon. Fear is a source of instability and hence it is important to understand fear, discuss different types of fears that bring instability, and see what some potential ways might be to absorb or abolish fear.

I already mentioned about Kartik being afraid of facing interviews. It was not that he did not know the material that the interviewers were going to ask him. And even if you don't know, it is not the end of the world. Well, he never realized that. Due to his fear of interviews, he kept working in the same bank in the same position without any promotion or a change of job for countless years of his prime. Internally he was certainly not happy because so many other employees that were his juniors and also whom he tutored for officer exams became officers. He was so much smarter than all of them but the only reason he did not dare to give the exam was that there would be an interview and he did not want to face it. Even when his boss asked him to apply for the exam he refused.

Fear has the power to derail the course of one's life. A derailed course is not one that all can be at peace with. For most, the derailed course of life is the one that they can never be at peace with and hence are in a perpetual state of radioactivity. Krupali is a student in high school but is so nervous during her Viva/oral exam that despite knowing the answer, she is not able to communicate it. She moved away from studying science and medicine because of this. She feared that if she was asked a question during her viva or her presentation at a conference or asked by a patient, she would not be able to answer it. Hence, she diverted her studies and life in a direction where she would not have to face questions.

Both Krupali and Kartik suffered from fears that most people on the planet fear too. The fear of public speaking is the number one fear on the planet. Even Mahatma Gandhi was afraid of speaking in public. He developed the ability to absorb it and ultimately, he did overcome his fear of speaking in public. If you come to think of it, globally fear of public speaking is a huge source of instability and radioactivity. I have surmized that fear of Public speaking is like a sunflower. Sunflowers are complex flowers that are made up of many smaller flowers. Fear of public speaking includes many smaller fears such as the fear of forgetting, fear of fumbling, fear of making mistakes, fear of disappointing others, fear of not meeting expectations, and more.

For innumerable people, the hour before they have to speak in front of the public is like a psychological world war where the other side is hell bent on exclusively using only radioactive weapons. It is a war that most don't win, and due to that loss, humanity loses learning the potentially rich and diverse viewpoints and nuances from fertile minds. In the case of job interviews, employers often miss out on hiring extraordinarily skilled employees who are naturally taciturn and are so afraid in their minds that they will refrain from articulating their thoughts. I reiterate that fear is a source of instability and radioactivity.

In an interaction with one of the leaders of the Vikram Sarabhai Community Science Center in Ahmedabad, India, it became distinctly clear to me that the fear of mathematics and science is not just specific to America. In India too, so many kids are afraid of math and science and hence make career choices avoiding math and science completely out of the fear of the subjects. In a nation that needs doctors badly to provide medical care to its 1.4 billion population, one of the reasons we don't have doctors and scientists is fear of math and science.I know for sure that you never made the connection between fear and the scarcity of scientists and doctors. Well, now you know so i request you to ensure that your own kids, nieces, nephews, and the children in your vicinity are not fearing math and science. There are many things you can do and if nothing occurs to you contact me. i will make sure that the child is helped.

Let me give you an overview of different types of fears that exist and make life living hell for those suffering from it. Jodi is a 71-year-old lady who has strictly stayed away from cotton for the last 55 years. She developed the fear of cotton when she was young and that fear has been with her forever. To be mortally afraid of cotton seems childish and unlikely but that is the puzzling reality for Jodi where she cannot effectively function due to it. Going to county fairs has been problematic for her because often times the stitching on the stuffed toys open and make the cotton inside visible. Due to her fear of cotton, pillows too initially scared her forcing her to sleep without pillows. While this all may seem fictitious, but then there are countless other fears that are even more bizarre than this one. There are documented fears of navel or belly button, coins, beard, number 13, and more. All this prohibits you from thinking or doing certain things. At times fears also motivate other individuals to bias and discriminate against such fearful individuals. Let's assume Jack is afraid of men with beards, it is likely that Jack will end up drafting workplace policies that are moderately unfair for bearded guys. After 9/11 there was a big stigma against keeping long beards while traveling internationally especially if you had to pass through borders where human officers were in charge of granting entry. There were several instances where fear led tothem being extra cautious, which led to them being likely discriminatory.

Jignesh is a 55-year-old employee of a nationalized bank in India and is a proud owner of a car. Since childhood it was his dream to own a car and be able to drive a car. To actualize his dream he worked diligently in a bank for 27 years to ensure that he was able to afford a car. Finally, he was approved for a loan and became an owner of a car. Despite it being his dream to own a car, he is not able to actualize the dream fully because he cannot drive it. Well, he has a driving license, and he is able to drive the car, but he has an unusual fear that prevents him from driving. He is afraid that as soon as he will drive his car on the road, an auto rickshaw will scratch his car. He is afraid that somehow a rickshaw will find his car like a guided missile and make a dash toward it.

This fear has prevented him from actualizing his dream of being a car owner and going on family picnics in his car. There is a unique fear of driving cars on highways, which I have seen in the Indian diaspora community in the US and Canada. My cousin who has lived in Texas for the longest time refused to drive her car on the interstate highways. So, she would not be able to go pick up or drop any guest from the airport who would be coming to her place. If she took the interstate, it would take her 45 minutes to reach the airport but if she took side roads then it would take her 100 minutes to get to the airport. She was just afraid of driving on the interstate.

My brother-in-law in Canada simply refuses to drive on the highways. He has developed fear due to a mishap once, which also happened to be his first time, and hence refuses since to drive on highways. Well, I can talk from my experience too that I met with an accident where a police car rear-ended me on an express highway between Ahmedabad and Vadodara in India. We were all safe and although we were rear-ended by a police car, we had to go through so much hassle that I just decided to not drive on Indian roads anymore. Part of the decision was influenced by fear of the legal complications that may arise if I ever got into an accident again. For two years I did not drive in India but then I worked with myself, defeated the fear, and began driving again on Indian roads.

I was mainly able to overcome my apprehension and fear with the use of logic and information. I told myself that accidents do happen but if accidents can be guaranteed and predicted accurately then they are not accidents but more of planned events. Nobody plans for accidents to happen, so all I have to do is to be a bit more careful and follow the rules. While this rationalization worked for me, the same rationalization was not going to help Jignesh or my cousin or my brother-in-law from overcoming their fears. While knowledge is the best way to dissolve fear there is no guarantee that knowledge will be effective. A certain cognitive fertility or eligibility is required for knowledge to work. Just as a curve is needed in a surface to store water and how water cannot be stored on a flat surface, knowledge without proper cognitive eligibility is not going to be of much help in saving one from fear.

Fear of Injections and syringes is yet another fear that many people in many countries have. Sylvia had this fear of syringes and injections. She became extremely nervous and lost her vitality before she has to do any blood tests. She was terribly afraid of the syringe. More often than not the pain from the syringe is made so much bigger and gruesome in the mind that the phrase making mountain out of a mole comes to life in this situation. People hyperventilate so much that they instantly transform into patients for no good reason. The times when COVID-19 was active became a nightmare for Sylvia. While everyone around her was rushing to get the vaccine, she kept averting it and avoiding it in the hope that a vaccine that she could consume through her mouth was around the corner. When she realized that this was not at all a possibility, she had to finally go and get injected with the vaccine. Nervousness and anxiety, in other words, instability stayed with her till after the time she actually got vaccinated. The 17 days she had to spend thinking about her brought her immense instability and radioactivity in her life. Since she is afraid of injections and wants to avoid them, another thing that she desperately stays away from is anything that is made of Iron. She is very nervous around anything made from Iron because if she is injured by it, she will be forced to take the Tetanus injection. To avoid taking Tetanus injections, Sylvia avoids anything made out of Iron. These are some extreme lengths that people like Sylvia go through and be perennially unstable to avoid one-time shot of injections.

Child trafficking is something I find totally and absolutely disgusting. To be a victim of it is one of the most destabilizing experiences. To be separated from your family or in worse cases being sold by the family and then be forced to have sex with countless unknown men every night for a major part of your life is a harrowing thought. When the thought itself is so destabilizing the actual experience is unfathomable. In many instances, young girls are married to guys in big city and then the husbands sell these girls to brothels. There was a popular culture movie about this in India which became a big hit. The name of the movie was *Gangubai Kathiawadi*. This movie brought to fore a story of an innocent small-town girl who was brought to Mumbai through marriage and then sold off. This movie released around the same time when the big National Geographic article titled "Stolen Lives" about how young girls were abducted from Durga Pujo and then sold to brothels had come out. Ironically, Durga Pujo is the biggest celebration of the female power in the nation.

Shiksha a girl in 11th standard who was failing to concentrate on her studies brought a somewhat related but also an entirely different and nuanced fear to my attention. During my session she revealed to me that she was eternally afraid that she might fall in love with the wrong guy who will then ruin her life. Here what she meant was that the wrong guy would not allow her to continue her higher studies or ban her from going to work and building a professional career. This guy could also not allow her to help her parents, which she badly wanted to since they needed it. This fear that she could fall in love with someone messed up had gripped her so strongly that every time Shiksha sat down to study, her mind would instantly wander in the fantasy land where her life was in ruins due to her falling in love with the wrong person. This brought her tremendous instability since she was neither able to perform well in her exams nor was she able to explain this fear to her parents. Some of this also goes to the earlier chapter about anxiety, fantasy, and injustice. Due to the fear of the what if she spent more time in fantasy and did injustice to herself before any actual injustice happened to her.

Arpita is a mother of an eight-year-old boy. They live in a safe gated society where there are 12 towers. Every evening hundreds of children come down to play in the common play area where they play different games such as cricket, football, Kho Kho, badminton and more. While everyone is playing downstairs, Arpita's eight-year-old boy Ved is sitting in the home. What is the reason for it? The reason for this is the clutching fear that Arpita has. Arpita has this irrational fear that as soon as Ved will go down and start playing, a big bus or truck will come at full speed and crush him. They live in a society where there is no way a vehicle or a person can enter without a prior and double-authenticated permission system. There is no way a bus or a truck can enter into the premises but still the price of her fear is paid by Ved who is deprived of physical activity and friendship. To reduce her instability arising from the fear Arpita has banned her children from socializing and playing with other children. If she was able to absorb her instability, then her children would have a normal upbringing just like hundreds of other children in society. Her radioactivity is maybe not damaging her because she is in charge but is certainly damaging her children and keeping them from an optimal environment to grow and flourish.

Veronique is 40 years old. She is afraid that she might say something which may not be appreciated by others. She is so afraid that she continues to live a subdued existence. She has never been herself or expressed herself truly and fully to her family because of her fear that what if something she says can hurt the sentiments of people around her. This has continuously been a source of unstability for her and because of that she has not been able to be fully happy. Her fear created serious day-today troubles for her and despite trying hard she has not fully been able to over come her fear.

After the COVID-19 pandemic, there is an elevated fear among the youngsters of losing their loved ones. Jay was a 19-year-old boy in one of my classes. He expressed that he had the fear of losing his parents and because of this fear and its related instability, he was often not able to focus on his studies or seldom enjoy sports. His mind would keep going back to thinking about the same thing again and again, no matter how much he tried to think of something else.

Once the class concluded, I asked Jay that will your fear prevent your loved ones from dying? He responded by saying that he fully well knew that him fearing or for that matter nothing else could prevent his parents from passing away at their destined time. Despite the knowledge, he was unable to escape the clutches of fear. In this unstable and radioactive state, his mind would keep imagining different scenarios that could cause his parents' death. Poor Jay did now know that his mind was getting a kick from this, and he had entered that dark chamber where darkness becomes the most unusual ally. While he did not know this fully, he was unable to imagine his life post the death of his parents. This kept the cognitive dissonance on. The disturbance in his mind was always on because he had built an opaque wall that did not allow him to see beyond.

The irony of fear is that other people's fears are often funny and laughable. In a household situation, a sister's or wife's fear of cockroaches or lizards is laughed at by the husband, and often times the husband's or brother's fear of pressure cooker whistling is laughed at by the wife or the sister. Other people's fears are also seemingly implausible and hence people regularly feel that the other people are making up fears until it is their time to share their personal brand of implausible fear. While others' fears are funny our own fears are never funny and debilitating. Fear brings in a very personal form of instability. While some of it is shared by many, there are some burdens that one has to carry alone. Regardless, whether the burden needs to be born individually or collectively, in the context of this book it is a global source of instability and radioactivity. It's just that the instances that I have shared thus far the radiation is experienced by the person or the people around that person.

There are many other fears such as the fear of heights, water, darkness, empty spaces, closed spaces, failure, ghosts, spiders, dogs, exams, and more that rule over the lives of people. Fear of loneliness or being alone is a tad bit paradoxical in an era that is singularly marked by individuality and enhanced privacy requirements.

Fear targets thoughts, actions, and decisions. Once under the influence of fear an individual is never free to make his or her own decisions. The influence of fear is such that it hijacks reason and ration and locks them up rendering an individual ineffective to discriminate between real and unreal. In other words, a person's Vivek (discerning ability) is lost. Abhayta is critical for Vivek and fear corrodes our Vivek. Fear is also the overpowering of the Vipritgyaan over the senses of a person.

I am convinced that fear is the nemesis of freedom. A human can never be free as long as he or she is influenced or dictated by fear. As a society we have to ask if we, our structures, our policies, and even our evolution and transformation are influenced by fear or something else. With so much violence and violent conflict/wars going on around the world, it is no rocket science to say that fear is at the root of these armed and violent conflicts. Fear of losing territory, fear of losing sovereignty, fear of losing culture, fear of aggression, and more are making nations behave irrationally subjecting hundreds of thousands of innocent women and young children to a premature death sentence. We have to learn to conquer and defeat our fears for a harmonious peaceful sustenance.

American Irony

The US is the number one country in the world. It is the superpower, the big brother of every nation on planet earth. Its military might is unparalleled. Its defense budget is larger than the next 15 countries combined. With vast resources, deep pockets, and military might, this country is one of the strongest on the planet. This might have given the people living in this country a stable chance to live life and flourish. I too have benefitted from this stability in the last 15 years. There is something I observed that I want to share, especially with my readers.

I am affiliated with Senior Centers in two cities. Senior Centers are these incredible government-sponsored facilities that afford countless opportunities to senior citizens to remain cognitively and physically active and be involved in funding things of their interest. Since fear is one of the areas that I do research in I would conduct workshops on fear for seniors. While there was a broad variety of fears that these seniors felt, one of them I thought was most intriguing. I reached out to the director and requested if I could do a specific workshop on that one particular fear. The director agreed. The topic was De-cluttering.

Cluttering has become an integral human trait. I was always taught that I am not going to take anything with me after my death so don't hoard or collect unnecessary things. Hoarding and cluttering has happened on steroids in the US. After the Second World War the increase in disposable incomes, culture of credit and financing, and the systematic encouragement of excessive consumerism ensured that the baby boomers and Gen X have ended up with so much clutter that it is unfathomable. These are all seniors now and with losing strength and agility, they are unable to keep up or maintain the clutter. What was once a prized possession is now poisonous and painful burden.

In the session I conducted on de-cluttering, most of the participants had their homes and in addition to their homes had 2–3 storage spaces rented for life. Can you believe that these individuals had 2–3 storage spaces because all that they had would not fit in their homes? Every month they paid rent money to hold on to all those things. The self-storage industry, which has emerged out of this need is estimated to be anywhere close to 30 billion dollars. While I thought this was ridiculous, I also sympathized because once in the middle of the year or during Christmas prep when they would go to these storages to bring back their ornaments, lighting, and other decoration material, they would be filled with melancholy seeing things that they had almost forgotten.

What I learned that day was that people are not only afraid of losing their loved ones, but they are even more emotionally attached to possessions and things. They are so afraid to break their own heart that they don't let go of things for which they don't have any space in their home. Their woe was that their kids didn't want anything to do with the things that they had been so meticulously preserving for decades. Their kids who are millennials and Gen Z don't even own homes to accommodate so much stuff. Moreover, the styles and fashions have changed so much that these kids also don't have an aesthetic liking for such things.

So many of the seniors were sad about their grandmother's China that they had so carefully preserved to pass on. Kids have no emotional connection to these things, so they ask the seniors to use them making all sorts of rational arguments that these are for using and they are not museum pieces. You have saved them and preserved them for such long, you now deserve to use them. In matters of emotional attachments, rational arguments don't typically succeed. Here too they were not succeeding.

This phenomenon is a mix of fear, anxiety, unhealthy attachment, and consumerism. All of this, while unique to the US will soon become a thing everywhere else too. If 1.4 billion Indians had the same average per capita belongings as the folks in the US, then clutter would become a globally intractable problem. Thanks to the ancient wisdom of India and continued adherence to it that the earth and humanity is in much better shape. If everyone became like the Americans with as many possessions and material objects, there would be no place for anything on earth.

Fear of what will happen to all these collected items was something that bothered my participants a lot. They could see that the last 40 years of hard work was going to go to trash or be destroyed. This gave them immense instability. Something even more interesting that came out from that session was that many individuals who have these storages were unable to pay rental fees of the units due to increasing health care costs or death. The ownership of these rental units is then reverted back to the owners of the storage facility. One of the TV channels has produced a TV show called Storage wars. The storage units are put to auction and there are professional bidders who will bid at every storage auction. If they win the bid, they get to keep everything that is in the storage unit. This way the storage unit is emptied, which makes it open for another person to rent it and also by selling or keeping the stuff from the unit the bidder can make some money. This show has also had multiple seasons. It was a reality TV show. You might be able to catch a few glimpses of it on YouTube. I found this entire thing incredibly ironic where what you have becomes a source of fear, agony, and instability.

Defeating Fear

If an individual is unable to defeat fear in the moment, then fear will influence and dictate many actions, thoughts, and decisions of that individual's life. Do note here that defeating fear in this book means enabling the inner strength to counter the force of fear and not letting it overwhelm or influence your thoughts, actions, or decisions.

Defeating fear does not mean becoming fearless. Defeating fear also does not mean eliminating or destroying the source of fear. What this means is that if a person is afraid of a spider, or in other words, if a spider is causing instability and radioactivity, we don't go ahead and kill the spider. In this case we can kill a spider since it's much weaker than us. Defeating fear is not about eliminating the spider's presence, it is about elevating your countervailing force so that you can withstand the presence of the spider without being influenced or dictated by it. In the moment when you come face to face with spider, if you are able to not be perturbed by its presence then it can be said that you have defeated fear of that spider.

I will highlight two tactics that one must do to cruise along on the journey of defeating fear by improving internal strength. The first thing one should do before applying the two tactics is to do a stock-taking. Take stock of your fears. Sit quietly for 10 minutes and think about all the things that make you fearful. Think of all the people, situations, instances, etc. that make you fearful, and write them all down in the space provided in the below box.

In Table 7.1, you will see that I have filled in my top 10 fears. Similarly, I give you the space in Table 7.2 for you to fill out your top 10.

There is no need to go further than ten at the moment. It is fine if you don't have ten and can only list less than ten. But there is no need to go beyond ten. It is important that you do this stock-taking. This will bring forth fears that

TABLE 7.1 10 Things that Inspire Fear in Me

What are 10 things that inspire fear in me?	
Water	*Deviation from the path of righteousness*
Darkness	Donating blood
Physical injury	Certain peculiar sounds
Insult	Dogs
Reintroduction of what habits I have given up	Losing control over my brain

TABLE 7.2 10 Things that Inspire Fear in You

What are the 10 things that inspire fear in you?

live in the shadows. Once you have completed this step then I request that you apply the first tactic that I am going to share here.

Guest or Host

With the list of your top 10 fears ready, it is now time to dive into analyzing them further into one of the two categories. Identifying and categorizing fears into one of the two categories is the first tactic for defeating fear. The two categories are guest or host. The essential question to ask here is whether fear is a guest or a host of your life.

A guest is someone who visits and goes away. A guest has limited power and limited influence. It is at times ok if one has to tolerate a guest. But that is not the case with a host. A host has unlimited power and exerts tremendous influence over the guest. If fear is a guest in our life, then we have more power over it. But if fear has become a host of our life, then it has more power over us than what should be the case. We have an uphill battle to defeat fear. So, in the space below identify and categorize which fears are guests in your life and which ones are hosts (Table 7.3).

See if you have more guests or more hosts. The goal here is to ensure that after an initial starting point we constantly move towards transforming more hosts into guests. And ultimately ending up with all guests upon whom you have more power. Now, for example, fear of darkness was a host of my life. It influenced a lot many of my social and interpersonal interactions as well as activities I participated in and did not. Once I identified that it was a host, I started working on transforming it into a guest with limited power. I can convincingly say that 9 out of 10 times I am able to kick the guest out of my life when I want. It has no grip over my life anymore. Identifying is the first step. So, take a look at your list and see how many guests you have and how many hosts you have.

TABLE 7.3 Guest or Host

Name of Fear	*Guest (Yes/no)*	*Host (Yes/no)*

First, kick the guests out. The way to do so is by realizing that they are guests and have no permanent power over you. You are their host. They rely on you to feed and exist. The moment you stop nourishing them they find it impossible to survive and exert their influence. Hosts, unlike guests, cannot be directly kicked out. If you try to do so, then they will generate too much instability and resulting radioactivity in your life. With them, you have to be gentle and tactful. The primary thing to do is to transform them slowly and surely into guests. When they start to exert pressure that is when you resist and with persistent resistance you transform them into guests and then kick them out. So, it's a two-step process.

Laughter is the Best Medicine

Fear completely and entirely ceases to exist in an individual when they are laughing out loud or rolling on the floor laughing. The sad reality of today is that both laughing out loud and rolling on the floor laughing happens only on texts. LOL and ROFL are seldom seen in daily lives. And even more rare in spaces where there is an absence of alcohol or other mind-numbing substances.

Think about the last time you were laughing out loud. Was there any existence of any fear in your system? The answer has to invariably be no. Fear temporarily disappears when one is laughing. The chemical constitution in the brain and the body is such at the time of laughter that fear has no space to exist. So, what am I suggesting here? Am I suggesting that you laugh all the time? Maybe, that's a way to defeat fear. But it might not be possible for everyone to do that. However, one thing that I have learned is that it is possible to fool your brain. I am not saying that it is going to be a cake walk but it can be done. Your brain can be trained to activate and develop a certain chemical constitution where fear has no space. When you realize that fear is taking over, you can momentarily put yourself in that laughing state where the chemical constitution will fight with the chemical constitution of fear. It's the fight between two opposing forces. No matter how much snow has accumulated, if the sun is shining bright it will have to slowly start melting. Similarly, no matter how strong of a host a particular fear is, the laughter-inspired chemical constitution will slowly and surely work to ensure that its grip is loosened and slowly the host is transformed into a guest, which is much easier to kick out.

Final Remarks on Fear

Fear is a motivator and an inhibitor, so many people do see merit in fear. I don't. I firmly believe that fear is something that brings instability and radioactivity in humans and humanity. If we were not afraid of people who don't look like us, the world would have been a much better place to live. That's one fear that has become host and looms over humanity. We also have a name for it. It's called Xenophobia: the fear of strangers and foreigners. How many times in your life a complete stranger has given you help when you didn't ask for it? How many times someone from your family was in an accident and some random strangers immediately rushed to help? There is a whole different side to the coin too, but we have to be reasonable and rational. We can't just hate or be afraid of everyone stranger and foreign. Fear is not ideal and is not required because anything motivated by fear is nothing but a seed of instability.

To reduce radioactivity, we have to defeat fear and absorb it deep within through our creative psyche for ensuring that the damage to other humans and humanity can be minimized. Defeat fear within and all around you.

8

DENOMINATORS OF HUMANITY

i ask you *my dear reader* that how many times in the previous six months were you in a situation where you didn't fully comprehend the meaning and relevance of events around you. i find it immensely common in people to not have a grasp of the many things that happen around them and within them. They fail to understand things around them because they don't really have an idea of the denominators. Denominators are like highways. You can keep driving on them without really understanding them. If you are driving for the sake of driving then it's great, keep driving. But if you have to reach a destination then the purpose is to choose the denominators or the highways that will get you to your destination. Denominators just like highways are not always simple to understand. More so when you try to make sense of them, they further don't make any sense. Some of the answers as well as the questions can be found in what i refer to as the Denominators of Humanity. Denominators of humanity are some common and shared traits by humanity. These denominators are ideally supposed to bring in harmony and stability and they also do that but more often than not they also become sources of instability and radioactivity in humans. I will give you a sneak peek into the fluid, unfair, unjust, unpredictable world of some selected denominators.

Morals, Laws, and Values of the mortal world

While preferred and popular, morality of the human world is fluid and inconsistent. This unfortunate fluidity, and inconsistency of morals, in itself, is a source of hopeless instability and subsequent radioactivity. Morals are not some set engravings on a stone. Simply put they are merely the agreements and consensus between groups of people. We rely on the stability of morals

DOI: 10.4324/9781032627564-8

to regulate our conduct. Agreements can change. People who have made those agreements can also change. Circumstances and situations can also change.

i often ask myself the following questions:

1 If morals stopped existing, what percentage of people will become wayward and unruly? And is that percentage going to be any higher or lower than the percentage of people that are currently wayward and unruly?
2 What is the cost we pay for being moral?
3 How much has immorality damaged human progress?
4 What does amorality bring to the table?

i am a big stickler about morals and values that result in compassion and kindness toward others. i am therefore also connected with an organization that works exclusively to strengthen the moral fabric of an individual and society. However, when i get exposed to the immorality of humans and human endeavors, i can't help but think that, in today's times, morals and values have sadly achieved the status of vestigial organs. Their presence or absence makes little to no difference to most if not all. Indifference toward them or in other words amorality is becoming prevalent. Do know that amoral is not immoral.

Also, what fascinates me is the hip and joint relation between morality and power. What is moral? What is ethical? What is legal? The sun might be shining up high but there still might be places such as valleys where despite shining up high the sunlight does not reach. Similarly, the same action can qualify to meet the criteria in all three categories of moral, ethical, and legal, and at the same time, it can meet only one criterion but not the other two criteria. The fluidity of agreements between groups of people is at the core of this. This chapter will elaborate on the neuroplasticity and flexibility required to absorb the instability.

i would argue at the risk of being easily disproved that when change was relatively slow, there prevailed some kind of moral stability in the lives of individuals. However, in the 21st century, the century defined by change and labeled as the agile era, there is lesser stability of morals and subsequently lesser morals in the lives of individuals. The change in technology and dynamics requires a quick turnaround of agreements on morals. However, before the new agreements reach the masses and become part of their conduct, there are newer technologies in place. People are finding it hard to keep up with the change and are therefore unfortunately giving up too. This is where the seeming apathy and amorality emerge from.

As a professor who teaches creativity, advertising, and mass media at a major global university, i got the front seat to witness a recent storm by the name of ChatGPT. This storm is an interesting one because it has brought morality back into the conversation. In universities and educational settings, the sun never sets on topics of morals, and values, and integrity. But it is these extraordinary events of moral eclipses such as ChatGPT that allow us to exclusively focus on considerations of and nuances of morality for a while before everyone starts turning a blind eye to them.

Once again as a professor, i get a front seat in the societal shifts pertaining to the use of pronouns. From the binary, he and she, to the inclusion of it and they and them as well as the inclusion of a broadening spectrum of gender preferences and choices morality has been tested. To refer to anyone with an accurate pronoun is preferable and the right thing to do. In this case, if you think carefully, the moral standard has not changed but the advances in apt references are not reaching the people as quickly. Moreover, if the new references reach the people they get caught up in social and societal quagmires ultimately delaying the adoption and increasing the agony of people on both and in this case all sides. This is in turn leading to the likely increment in the extant radioactivity of the people on all sides.

And the attachment that we develop toward morals is also another issue, and where does that take us? Why do we get attached to systems of morals? Well, it is because they have yielded certain results wherein it has allowed us to live peacefully, and it has allowed us to exist in harmony in many ways. But is there a possibility where we can rethink the entire system of morals not just to make it more time relevant or maybe less anachronistic. So, what would be an alternative to the system of morals or to the system of agreements? How can we live without that common code? This is something for the classrooms to spend time as a thought experiment. However, in this chapter we won't highlight how the changes in the moral code result in a different understanding altogether of how we conduct ourselves.

Along with morals, there are also ethics and values and laws. When laws are concerned, many times we borrow understanding from hard sciences. This is because laws are unchangeable and unshakable in all contexts of lives. But that is not true for social sciences because in social sciences we don't have everlasting laws since we don't have such stable relations that always behave in the same ways. Even the formation of societies was based on laws that we uphold. There are provisions to amend laws because with time and changing sensitivities things that were legal become illegal. The US has fought fiercely against certain practices which were legal in a certain time period on the grounds of morality. In the end morals or rather morality has emerged victorious, and the laws were amended to support and side with morality. Culmination of the Civil War and the culmination of the Civil Rights Movement brought relief to so many by curbing down immoral not illegal practices.

Laws become the source of radioactivity, and let me give two examples from the US and one from the UK. If you live in the US then depending on the state you are living in, you can and cannot be topless. There are something like 19 different definitions of nudity and what constitutes as nudity. If found not following these, you can be arrested and penalized. Also, the severity of punishment is different in different states. Such fluidity and discrepancy cause instability. In the US, anybody under the age of 21 is not allowed to consume alcohol. Regardless of age, one is not permitted to carry open containers of alcohol outside of a designated establishment. Well, these are the laws. And most people abide by them and live by them. However, when I was leading a group of undergraduate students in Italy. The laws there were very different. The minimum drinking age was 18 and there is no open container law as well. Anybody above the age of 18 was allowed to drink and even carry alcohol freely while consuming it in the middle of a road. My students from the US felt really liberated for those few weeks and many even expressed their desire to move to Italy due to this law.

Laws and policies can be changed, amended or abolished. Although they can have a substantial impact on the lives of people. My example from the UK is about Brexit, a drama that ensnared the imagination of millions across the globe. Britain or some Britishers decided to not be a part of the European Union since they saw less benefit in it and felt like they were contributing a lot more to subsidize many things for others when their own people were struggling. A general election was held, and a majority of people voted for Britain to exit, and it did. Britain ceased to be a part of the EU. This change in law inspired by Brexit required so many subsequent changes, which made life different if not challenging for many. Brexit brought stability to many pushing for it and instability to those who were against it. It is possible that in five years Britain will decide to become a part of the EU. My point here is that laws are fluid and transient. Some have a longer life and some are very short. Nonetheless, their impact on instigating radioactivity cannot be ignored.

Come to think of it, was the practice of colonizing moral or immoral? The world as well as the world order must have changed so much because of the colonizing practices. The very nations that vehemently protected their white picketed fences were the ones that went all around the world and breached the sanctity of the invisible fences of other guest loving nations. The drawing and the redrawing of boundaries cause so much radioactivity. What is currently happening between Israel and Palestine is an example of it. What is currently happening between Russia and Ukraine is an example of it.

Morals, Laws, and Values of the Spiritual World

Ignorance is bliss. I am sure you have heard this phrase. It's true and it's false at the same time. A state of bliss or indifference can come through ignorance. Indifference emerging from ignorance is short lived and unstable in itself. Indifference is stable and permanent when it emerges from the illumination of enlightened knowledge. Things work differently in that plane of existence.

What we need to understand here is that things such as policies, territories, affiliations, loyalty, and laws might be fluid and prone to change. Morality of the human world does not apply as is to the spiritual world is what i have learned from my time in Madhuban Ashram, situated in the foothills of the Himalayas. The discrepancy between the rules of the moral world and the spiritual world may be the reason why we don't understand the many things that happen around and within us, including radioactivity. But when understood through the right kind of perspective and interpretations, these very same fluid morals and wisdom transform in righteousness-inspired action plans. This is also when you realize that fluidity is not actually a source of radioactivity instead it is a provision that is in place to get closer to flourishing. However, for such counterintuitive wisdom to dawn, it takes time, it takes guidance, it takes a little bit of experience, it takes a little bit of practice. We are so used to seeing fluidity as a source of pain and agony that now it takes us immense patience and perseverance to see it otherwise.

What I mean over here is that without the fluidity of morals it is impossible to create and curate a path that is optimal for a being in a given lifetime. There are so many things that a person can do however the only thing that an individual, a human being, should endeavor to do is to seek liberation through enlightenment. Now if rigidity were the only way to get there, it would exclude a large part of humanity. There is a provision for fluidity to ensure that everyone who does not have the needed eligibility to choose one path can resort to their path. Such an understanding-rich attitude is required to be cultivated through learning and knowledge.

There are four types of grace that are required to develop the attitude, which sees fluidity as a provision and not as an obstruction or an instigator of radioactivity. These four graces are the grace of a guru, the grace of the divine, the grace of the scriptures, and the grace of the self. Without all of these, it is practically impossible to cultivate and foster understanding with the right attitude.

Our life unfortunately revolves far too much around the morality of the petty human world. Our life revolves far too much around the petty laws and policies of the human world. Well, there is nothing wrong in it because we are humans, so it is only right that our lives keep revolving around these things. Our lives will definitely not revolve around the laws and policies and norms of the animal world. As humans we have been afforded the prized intellect to go a little further, to go a little higher, and also bother ourselves with the rules and morals of the divine world, of the godly world. Everything works very differently over here. The equations of the divine world, the laws of that world, and the policies of that world are diverse, disproportionate, and unbelievably entangled for outsiders like us. Until we make deliberate attempts with the help from the above-mentioned four graces bestowed upon us, we don't really have a shot at understanding most of these things.

Coming back to the mortal world, the change that came along with Brexit did affect many people. It affected people not living there to some degree, and to a great degree to people living there. Ideally, such things should not occupy the entire mind space and become the exclusive source of instability and the resulting radioactivity for the people of that nation. But it did and many are still unhappy and living a very unpleasant life being mad and disgruntled about the fact that Brexit happened. All of these things that I mentioned such as the changes in the policies and the changes in the laws and so on and so forth affect the ones that are unprepared and the ones that are myopic. However, to the one who has the ability to think long term and has spent a significant amount of time in preparing oneself these are not the things that will perturb or bother him. A radioactive and unprepared individual is a big danger to society. And the basis for this can only be understood if you are a little bit well-versed with the rules and functioning of the spiritual world.

The rules and morality of the human world do not apply "as is" to the spiritual world and vice versa is something to always be remembered. This is a hard and challenging radioactive aspect preventing flourishing. Let us look at four other denominators of humanity.

Nafo... Nuksaan... Faydo...Setting...

I have been studying human behavior at the individual level as well as at the macro level. As a social scientist I keep a close watch on humanity to distill and parse out major thought movements, big themes, and unique oddities. I have lived for extended periods in several cultures and observed minutely the different drivers of cultures and humanity therein. Through intrinsic perceptiveness, I was able to broadly categorize a very large portion of human behavior into four categories.

There was a need to label these categories and while I tried many different permutations and combinations, finally I found the best labels in my mother tongue (Gujarati). It is believed that you are best able to articulate some of the most complicated and complex ideas in your mother tongue. And that was true in this particular case. I kept thinking and searching for four labels in English, but none really fit well but then when I started thinking in Gujarati, it instantly clicked. Nafo, Nuksaan, Faydo, and Setting came to me and surprisingly three of them were in Gujarati and the fourth one although in English is an accepted usage very much a part of the Gujarati language.

These four have become the default wirings of brains in the 20th and 21st centuries. To much dismay of mine, everything, every decision and every conversation, keeps revolving around these four. This chapter is about you because it will highlight the basic and fundamental behaviors of humans that constantly work to move humans away from stability and towards radioactivity. Although desirable, stability does not feed the shallow requirements of humans. On the contrary, it is this unexplainable need for instability that feeds him and fuels him.

Based on the extensive research of instability within a human being that I have conducted, I am convinced that the ancient folks were much smarter than us. They figured out human behavior and psyche long back. They knew more about us than we know. They had their finger on the real pulse. They must be so knowledgeable that they identified these pitfalls even wrote scriptures about them and how to avoid being trapped by them. But despite all the knowledge and understanding that prevails, we are not able to escape the clutches of these evils.

It is said that a wolf is fed by its legs. Just as how a wolf has four legs, here too there are four legs that drive an individual away from stability while constantly bringing him or her the illusion of stability. These four legs that drive us away from stability are nothing but a temporary illusion. I will elaborate on each of the four categories in this chapter and in the end conclude with how they move an individual away from stability.

Nafo (Profit) and Nuksaan (Loss)

A calculating mind is a cursed mind. There is no respite. A calculating mind does not allow a human to be in peace. A calculating mind keeps constantly nudging an individual that whatever he or she or they are up to is either worth it or not worth it. And a human like a conditioned dog keeps doing things that are worth it and keeps avoiding things that are not worth it.

Profit and loss are major controlling drivers of human behaviors. We, humans, are risk-averse and favor profit over loss. However, loss is not always bad, and profit is not always good. More of one thing is good is a very singular and myopic calculation. There are many variables that need to be considered to make such a determination. Loss of enemies is preferable over the gain of enemies. Loss of weight for an overweight person is a victory. They even had a reality TV show by the name "Biggest Losers." The show was about highly obese individuals who had lost unbelievable amounts of weight. The biggest loser was the real victor. Some of these individuals lost weight equivalent to the weight of two fully grown humans.

Evolutionary biology can give us a good understanding about why we favor profit over loss. We must look at and study the ancient times when our brains were getting wired. If you begin to wonder what the most important event in one's life, and the answer you would most likely arrive at is childbirth. For thousands of years, when modernity did not exist, when commerce and market were almost non-existent, the one event that was most magical and high impact was childbirth. The addition of a child, the gain of a child, the profit of a child was a tremendous source of joy. Secondary to that when one acquired more land, when one acquired more cows and buffalos, when one had access to more fruits, all it meant was that the person was secure and an able provider. Losing a child, losing a calf, losing a piece of land, and losing food was a source of deep pain and agony. This conditioning must have kept getting reinforced for thousands of years. And now we have a more than likely clear understanding and implications of profit and loss. Profit is good and loss is bad.

Humans are often seen to take risks to get more profit. They are not as often seen to take risks to avoid loss. We are perennially calculative. As if one curse was not enough, a theory was floated at some point that networking is the key. Every person you met was either a source of future profit or a source of future loss. The pros and cons of meeting a person, initiating a relation, maintaining a relation, deciding the best time to capitalize on your relational investment are what we end up thinking or rather calculating about. Our brain gets a kick out of analyzing and calculating whether a person is of use to you or not. Our brain enjoys its utilization and hence it keeps this cycle going.

Let me caution that not every form of profit and loss calculation is counterproductive. My argument is that profit and loss calculation in everything is counterproductive. In the ultimate pursuit of human life, which is liberation and emancipation the nafo and nuksaan mindset is paramount. But that's where it should end. The understanding of what actions and what utilization of human intellect will yield profit as they endeavor toward liberation is needed and even encouraged. Profit here is the inching closer to the destination and nothing else. The issue comes when this same understanding is applied to each and every aspect of material existence. This creates a vortex of instability and consumes a person. This is what needs to be avoided. i want that my readers become aware of this distinction.

Faydo

"Is me mera kya fayda?" translated into English as "What's in it for me?" is commonly heard wherever you go. Faydo or benefit, if you come to think of it, has become a major motivator of every human behavior. Such conditioning and maybe even obsession with benefit makes me sad because if there is no benefit there is no action. Corruption is a good example of this. Until the person is not getting something from you, he or she or they will not do the work that they are supposed to do and are also being paid for by their respective employer.

I have a story from my aunt's life experience that might help you understand this better. My aunt retired after decades of being a university professor. The education department had to process her retirement benefits. A year passed by, and nothing happened. She decided to go and check on the status of her file. She went to the education department and enquired about who was the respective office in charge she should meet to enquire about this. She was told that she should meet a Mr. XYZ. She goes up two floors and enters an office where there are many workers working in their respective cubicles. There were no name tags to identify who is who. So, she approaches one of the gentlemen and asks politely, "Hello, can you please tell me which one Mr. XYZ is?" Curtly, that gentleman replies, "What do you need from him?" My aunt says that it's been a year since her retirement, and she has not started receiving her pension. Her funds are depleting and wants to enquire on the status of her pension file. To this remark, the gentleman says, "Mr. XYZ is on holiday today, you can come tomorrow." Well, what can you do if the person you are supposed to meet is on leave? Nothing. So, my aunt returned home. Now understand the geographical situation here. My aunt lives in a city that is 250 km away from the city where the education department is. She has not been paid her pension for a year. She has to spend a good deal of money to travel and it's a whole day affair to go and come back. Anyway, that day was a waste because the person is on holiday. So, she left thinking of returning the next day.

She did not go the next day. She decided to hold her visit by a week. After a week she again took the long trip to the education department. She goes up the two floors to the same office and asks someone walking out of the office that where can she find Mr. XYZ. The person walking out pointed to the same guy my aunt has met a week ago. So, my aunt said, "no no he is not Mr. XYZ, is there another Mr. XYZ who was on holiday last week." The worker said,

> Madam, he is the only person in this division with that name. Seeing you he must have realized that there was not much to benefit from you, so he made you go round in circles. Quietly offer to pay him 2000–3000 Rs. he will get your work done.

No benefit, no work. No benefit, no appreciation. No benefit, no significance. This is the state of affairs and things. I keep imagining that the situation must be so ironic for my aunt when she must have been told that the very person she was looking for told her that he is on leave. What a terrible depletion of morals and values. And what was the reason? Mr. XYZ did not see himself benefitting from my situation since she had already remarked that her funds were depleting.

When I was doing an exclusive workshop on Fear for European business leaders, one thing I learned from them was that they had to introduce a new item line in their accounting ledger. This new item line was called "cost of doing business." It didn't occur to me how beautiful things and our world can seem with the use of euphemisms. All this new line item meant was that these businesses had to pay bribes to corrupt officers in certain parts of the world to get things done. Now bear in mind that most things that were shared were things that should have been done without any additional expenditure. For example, if a foreign company wants to register the company in a different country, they just have to fill out the form and ensure that all the legal requirements are met. That was not enough. Unless the officials were given motivational lubricants (money), they would not approve it under countless creative excuses. But as soon as the motivational lubricants were introduced work happened at warp speed. This is just to get the legal stuff done. I can even imagine the kind of moral poverty that may be seen in asking for illegal things and providing those illegal things. Sadly, morally decrepit behavior is normalized by making it a line item in the accounting ledger. All due to greed and benefit-seeking behavior.

Benefit-seeking behavior makes us do things that are not always aligned with our core behavior. Initially, it encourages you to make micro-compromises with your dignity and as time passes none of it is left. You become shameless. Shamelessness may not sound as bad, but it is. All humans more or less conduct themselves on the basis of shame. Deviation from righteousness might bring shame to them is what produces guardrails for human conduct. Incessant benefit-seeking behavior removes these guardrails. You lose a whole lot of your humane essence. I reiterate that a mind that calculates about everything is unfortunately a cursed mind.

My niece was going to leave for higher education. As a parting advise, i said the following to her. "There are no calculations in relations. If you keep the calculation of how much you have done and how much the other person has done for you, and what benefit you have derived from them then the relation will never be happy. A relation is about giving without keeping the count of the profit or the benefit that you can receive from a person. You give and sometimes even bend your back because it is your duty to do so. In return you don't deserve anything as your right in exchange for what you did as your duty. Relations, if you want them to flourish should not be transactional or calculation based." i don't know how much you would agree with what i said or not and its fine if you don't agree but this is what i shared with my niece as a parting advise. If you like some or all of it, you are welcome to use it as you please.

When i look at Faydo from a macro perspective, i feel that being driven by it reduces us humans to mere animals. Just as a dog does a trick for a treat, humans also do all kinds of tricks for the treat of benefit. Being imprisoned in the trick-for-a-treat cycle is heartbreaking. Here i would like to address you my dear reader directly and request that you catch yourself by the collar and lift yourself out of this swamp. Being stuck here is not a fine place because there are many better places to be.

Setting

Setting is a code word for shortcut. Setting is very commonly used in many parts of India. Jugaad is another word for it. In other countries and other cultures, they have different words for such shortcuts. So many things on the planet work through setting.

My problem with setting is when an individual exclusively relies on it for everything. It cripples the individual not allowing them to be free, independent, or confident. For everything people require settings. Your son or daughter wants a driving license. You go around asking people if they have any setting that will get their child a driving license regardless of their ability and eligibility to drive. If you want admission into a school for your toddler, you start asking around if there is any setting to get the admission. You want to go to a temple; you start asking around if there is any setting for VIP darshan. Setting might be good and may make your life simpler at times but they are sparsely and unjustly sprayed over humans. While all or let me say most humans seek settings, not all have the privilege or luxury of having them. And the not having of a setting causes more instability than the deficit of not having things that you need those settings for.

To not have settings is one cause of instability. Well, it is a huge problem when the setting that you have does not work like it should. Settings are short-cuts and they don't work all the time. Shortcuts can also be bumpy and unpleasant. Let me tell you the story of Gadlawala and Madhav. I have changed the names here for obvious reasons. Madhav was my friend growing up. He is still a friend. When Madhav passed his 12th standard exams with 86%, he desired to get admission in L.D. Engineering College of Ahmedabad. L.D. Engineering College is a reputed government-run and university-affiliated engineering college. Madhav had secured a good score, but he did not qualify by a percentage or two to be in the stream of engineering that he wanted to get into. Madhav started looking for setting to get into L.D. Engineering and into the stream of his choice.

Through some connection, my friend Madhav was put in touch with Gadlawala. Gadlawala was some guy who apparently had another setting in the ministry. After long discussions and evaluations of the strength of the setting, they reached a conclusion. While Madhav's single point connection was Gadlawala but based on a string of settings of Gadlawala Madhav was suggested to go and get admission in an engineering college that was 10 hours away by road. Based on the alchemy of Gadlawala's settings, it was possible for him to get Madhav transferred into the stream of his choice from a fara-way remote college but not from the same college into a different stream. His setting apparently did not have the clearance to change the stream but had the clearance and authority to change colleges. Happily, Madhav went to the engineering college far away and would come back once a month. When the first year was about the end, Madhav contacted Gadlawala. Gadlawala was not responding. Madhav tried several times but to no avail. How could he respond because he was dead. Gadlawala had died a natural death and my friend Madhav was now stuck in that far-off college. He had to spend one more year there in that college until he found another setting, which eventually got him transferred. My point here is that settings are unpredictable and hence make people radioactive. They are also unfair and hence one should rely on their own self and ability much more than their settings.

Conclusion

Denominators of Humanity are levers at both the macro and the micro levels. They can nimbly pivot the societal functioning and systems in favor of flourishing or in favor of radioactivity. My goal of introducing them to you is so that regardless of how the forces try to turn them you can flourish despite the radioactivity.

9

THE DURYODHANA SYNDROME

The title of this chapter is a verse from the epic, Mahabharata. Duryodhana, who is the leading antagonist of the epic, says the following lines "*Janami dharmam na cha me pravrttih, janamyadharmam na cha me nivrttih*," which make up the Duryodhana Syndrome. What he basically says is that "I know what behavior is righteous, but I am unable to persuade myself to do it. I also know what behavior is not righteous, but I cannot prevent myself from doing it." His helplessness brought upon the downfall of his family and along with them death of hundreds of thousands on the battlefield of Kurukshetra, an ultimate and fatal version of radioactive fallout.

Behavioral helplessness abounds us, which in turn elevates our instability and subsequently increases our radioactive potential. Ideally, if one knows that fire will burn his or her hand, then he or she will knowingly not put their hand in fire. But with behavioral helplessness we see numerous behaviors that are like deliberately putting one's hands in fire. This chapter will highlight some of the habits, compulsions, impulses, traits, and behaviors that constantly work to move a human away from stability. Emotional and behavioral hijacking through the nullification of wisdom is, whether you like it or not, a thing.

Our behavior gets hijacked, and we lose control over them. How many times has it happened with you that after a hissy fit, you tell your friend or mom that you have no idea what came over you because that is not you. This is what is referred to as behavioral and emotional hijacking. You behave erratically and unlike yourself in a given moment with no control over your thoughts or actions. Sometimes these lapses come with a heavy penalty. Such behavioral helplessness is problematic as far as living amiably in a society is

DOI: 10.4324/9781032627564-9

concerned. What needs to be understood is that this is a natural way to shirk off instability and return to a stable state. This is what being radioactive and radiating means.

Although desirable, stability does not feed human pride, greed, and ego. It is the unexplainable need for instability that fuels it. To give a small example, i am referring to the urges that awaken in an individual who sees a perfectly still water body. Instantly, a thought crosses my mind of what will happen if i throw a stone, how will it get disturbed. Similarly, when a kid is walking and sees an animal or a bird sitting perfectly still and enjoying its Zen moment, then there is an unexplainable urge within the kid to surprise and frighten the animal or throw a stone at it and ultimately disturbing the animal's Zen moment. YouTube and TikTok are full of such videos with a large following and viewership base.

My teacher shared with us in his class something that his teacher used to tell them. He said that as long, "As long as you are working on and struggling for survival, then the unconscious irrational urges and compulsions remain unmanifested. Once assured of survival, then the unconscious urges and compulsions manifest." This is a profound insight into the human conduct. In essence, assurance of survival is the much-awaited rain which brings to life all the wildflowers of the Death Valley in California. i don't even need to go as far as California, i can simply talk about my society where i have lived for more than 25 years.

We have a playground in the middle of the society with a cement pitch. Of course, the pitch is much needed since that is where we play cricket. For most of the year this place is dry, dusty, and sandy. But as soon as the monsoon arrives, from God knows where a lot of green starts showing up. Different varieties of plants and grass start growing. And they grow furiously, as if there is no tomorrow. Where were all these hiding until now? Well, they were always there in the ground. Safely stored away is the unconscious of the playground. As soon as their survival is assured after the rains, they start manifesting. What lies beneath us and inside of us is something most of us are entirely oblivious to. It's like you have no idea how a person is going to behave and react just when the influence of anesthesia starts wearing away. With some short essays and reflection pieces about some traits, compulsions, and impulses, i will present to you some of the legs that feed the wolf of radioactivity.

Point of NO Return

> i knew what i was doing was not right. Deep down i had an ill feeling. But still, i could not control myself. i, myself, don't know what overcame me and took over. It was like it wasn't even me. i would never do anything like this.

Most things that a person endures after moving beyond the point of no return are largely unpleasant and not ideal. So, what are the circumstances, rationalizations, explanations, reasons, and troubles that push a person beyond the point of no return? The point of NO return is something that we hear about often in trial courts. It is not spoken in the exact phrasing of the point of no return unless it is used by the legal counsel but when an amateur or a person without legal training speaks, it mostly sounds like the in quotes paragraph above.

i served for three years in what was then known as the University Conduct Committee (UCC). UCC was one experience that brought me face-to-face with the victims of behavioral helplessness and resulting radioactive disasters. These were individuals (young students) that simply could not deal with the instability and ultimately had succumbed to moving beyond the point of no return. Their radioactive fallout had reached a point where an external blunt force was needed to put an end to the harm it was causing to them, their targets, and the people around.

As a member of UCC, i underwent rigorous training to understand the nuances of the proceedings and the purpose of the proceedings. Although fashioned like a court of law, this was not a court of law and the whole purpose of this committee was not to penalize students and suspend them. It was to identify ways to make them realize where they went wrong and give them an opportunity to correct their behavior.

For a UCC member, the university would block 3-hour time slots, and depending on the stage of the process, these proceedings would be completed in 2 or 2 and a half hours. But then there were days when the entire proceeding would last much longer. Ideally, once you commit to be on a case, you only have a start time. There was no end time for the proceeding. i recall one proceeding where the committee along with the perpetrator and defender remained in the room for way longer than three hours. We all were let go after one of the parties had to be unfortunately taken to the emergency room on a stretcher.

i bring up this experience of mine because when seated on the other side, which is the judging side, a part of you constantly goes like, "how dumb can you be? It clearly says in the student code of conduct that you are not permitted to use the hair dryer in the dorm rooms because the fire alarms will detect it. And still you used it. If you are so dumb, then you deserve the punishment." This is exactly the urge that committee members most often need to fight vehemently against. And this is why we also have to undergo extensive training. The training does not make it easy; it is still hard because within your mind a conclusion is made based on the path of the least resistance.

A quickdraw conclusion clearly surmises that a student did not follow conduct rules, which are clearly laid down in the code of conduct, and therefore is guilty. The absolute need to not follow this path of least resistance, until a larger body of evidence and circumstances is studied, generates instability within the committee members. To put yourself in a situation where you have all the reason to conclude and stabilize internally but you still don't is anything but easy. This reminds me of what Prof. Rajmohan Gandhi said that when you have every reason to be angry, you instead forgive. This is when the chain of hatred is broken. Similarly, when you have every seeming reason to conclude, but you don't, this is when the chain of pseudo-justice could be broken. It is likely.

Let us move out of legal and conduct hearings and move on to some other aspects of life. i want to share a recent experience that i went through, which for a while became a source of immense instability within me. i love water but i am a pathetic swimmer. Thus, i've always kept a safe distance from water whenever needed and possible. i am even cautious when i am in the bathroom. Obviously not from the fear of sinking but from the risk of slipping.

One summer, i was in Switzerland. i was supposed to meet a friend in Bern and from there we were going to travel to his place in Neuchatel. He had called me the night before and asked that i bring my swimming trunks. The next morning, we both met, and i was carrying my swimming trunks. i had briefly toured Bern the day before with another group of friends where we saw the river Aare. Aare is a beautiful river of glacier water coming down the mountains meanderingly, and surrounding Bern.

My friend suggested that we do a walking tour. We did a walking city tour, which was a great experience. And also, something i would highly recommend. We visited several beautiful landmarks including the apartment in which Albert Einstein stayed. As the walking tour neared the Aare, the tour guide specifically mentioned that although, the famous summer activity in Switzerland is jumping and floating in rivers, and people all over the nation jump in rivers and then float in them for miles and miles. However, Aare is a very dangerous river, and you should jump in it only if you are an expert swimmer. She further added that Aare is a bit complicated because it flows at speeds of more than 20 km/hr. This makes it challenging to navigate. Everything happens very quickly including bad things. There could also be whirlpools due to the meandering of the river that require specialized skills to navigate. Moreover, since it is all glacier water, the temperature of the water is almost freezing, substantially increasing the risk of hypothermia. In my mind, i thought only fools would do such things like jumping in a raging river and thinking so i walked away from the river.

Two hours later, i found myself in the same frigid water holding onto a beach ball dearly for my life and calling out desperately to my friend to rescue me. i came very close to becoming the next victim of Aare. i am so thankful to my friend for rescuing me because, without him, i would have drowned. He was hurt much more than i was. He had external injuries and bloody injuries. Mine were internal and psychological. My injuries started manifesting a day or two later making the next 10 days painful and incredibly limiting. The psychological trauma of undergoing a near-death experience weighed heavy on me. Luckily, i was scheduled to attend a 5-day conference on Healing Wounds of the Past two days after the experience. That and sharing my experience with two wise individuals helped me work through my trauma effectively and conclusively.

i was no match for the river even when i was standing 500 meters away from it. Once in the water, i was a lamb tied to a post in front of a T-rex, waiting to be gobbled up alive. At this point, i would like to repeat.

> i knew what i was doing was not right. Deep down i had an ill feeling. But still, i could not control myself. i, myself, don't know what overcame and took over. It was like it wasn't even me. i would never do anything like this.

i really don't know what overcame me because i am not an adventurous kind and in my entire life, i have been especially careful with water. Moreover, being from the cultural background that i am where we have abundant access to astrologers, two astrologers had warned me with conclusive absoluteness to stay away from water because water is not my friend. One could say that i already had a toxic relation with water, but i was in denial until this moment. Despite the numerous yellow and red flags, i did not course correct, and i came close to losing my life because of it. Even while i sit here in the Blasco Public Library in Erie overlooking the tall ship USS Niagara and the Lake Erie, the traumatic flashbacks from my time in the river Aare are vivid and scary.

It is difficult to explain the overpowering feeling that snatches your agency to be in charge of your thoughts and actions. The questions that should arise before unfortunately arise after one has crossed the point of no return and those questions seem and look like: why did i do it? How could i have done this? Forget doing how could i have even thought of this? What was the need to do something like this? i created so much instability and radioactivity for me in such a short time. Fortunately, in this case, other than physical pain for 10 days there was no prolonged instability. But the psychological damage to many who suffer from such events brings in tremendous instability and if they are unable to manage the instability then it can also result in radioactive fallouts.

Let me talk about my friend, who is a high-ranking executive in a Fortune 200 company. He is very well respected in his field and is one of the most stable and wise persons that i know.

One day, while we were having an in-depth conversation, he shared with me this one incident, which shocked me. He told me that Arpan, i don't know what got into me this one time that before i realize anything, i caught myself driving at an unimaginable speed of 230 to 250 km/hr on the highway. He said that i am the kind of guy that drives 5 km slower than everyone else, and here i find me blazing at a dangerous lightning speed.

i still cannot come to terms with the fact that how could this gentle, loving, gem of a person do this? He mentioned that with driving he was trying to reclaim something that was lost. It was a fancy luxurious car with multiple airbags and there was a loud music. Music can do a number on your senses and rationality. Dancing is an example of it. Why does music make us dance? Why do we not dance otherwise?

Another individual shared with me that when younger, he one day set the kitchen, in his home, on fire. He knew it was not the right thing to do but he still anyhow went ahead and did it. i asked him if he had done this again or repeatedly. He denied saying that this was one of a kind of a thing. i just kind of wanted to see what happens. Oh, and he said once the kitchen was on fire, i ran out and then came back in and indulged in staged shouting that there is fire in the kitchen to get the attention of the elders in home. Thankfully, everyone was safe and the damage was repairable.

Hierarchy and greed can also create a certain point of no return, from where people are unable to turn back. The point of no return is a scary place because here you lose your agency and control. Many great and strong people have been victims of the point of no return.

Who Do i Belong to?

Belonging is a basic need of humans since we are inherently social animals. We all need and want to belong. We become sad and unhappy if we are made to believe that we don't belong. When a child misbehaves, or an adult commits a crime they are punished and forced to spend time alone where they temporarily don't freely belong to the mainstream.

i often think about who all do i belong to? What needs to happen or change in me for me to belong to someone? Do i belong to one or some or none or all? Is belonging a matter of norm or is it an outlying behavior?

Belonging also extends to things such as ideas, institutions, philosophies, ideologies, thoughts, friends, etc. What is it that i belong to is an area where one desires clarity. The lack or absence of clarity about belonging is a potent destabilizer. This is when i initiated an enquiry to see if i have clarity on who do i belong to, and what are other areas necessary for exploration of belongingness?

On the surface of it, i belong to my family, my relatives, some of my friends, my hobbies, my interests, and more. But on a deeper level, i feel that i strongly belong only and only to my values. i belong to my thoughts and words and actions. My belonging is to the highest ideal. Oh yes, i also belong to myself and my aloneness in this world. It is not a matter of shying away or eschewing responsibilities but a matter of raw reality that i came alone in this world and will go alone.

Moreover, i also feel like i should belong to all those who wish to belong to me. But this is where i run into some issues. All the above are entities that i have a favorable disposition towards. In other words, i love my parents and relatives and friends. i am fond of my values and thoughts and actions. But when it comes to belonging to the ones who wish to belong to me, i am not as good and unconditional about this as i should or maybe could be. i find that i am selective in who i want to belong to and what i belong to but more importantly who i let myself belong to. Why do i do this? Is it because of a bias or some kind of emotional hijacking? Maybe, it is a bias that prevents me from belonging with certain individuals who want to belong with me.

When we are made to feel that we don't belong, that is a potent source of radioactivity. Alternatively, when you are made to feel that you only belong to one group and are not allowed to belong to any other or many, then this too is a source of instability and radioactivity. Middle schoolers and highschoolers, in the US, often become victims of such forced belonging and eschewing. i did not study in the American system, so i am not aware of the different groups, but cliques do get created due to social pairings such as the popular kids, the marching band and music kids, the athletes, the anime followers, the nerds, sororities and fraternities, and more. Many times, kids are forced to belong to one or the other when they don't necessarily want to, and this is something that gives rise to instability and radioactivity in the child.

Belonging with a set of individuals who have been sexually active as opposed to those who are not is another distinction that is a major source of radioactivity in young adults. Virginity or the lack of it becomes a major point of judgment and acceptance in social groups. Consumption of alcohol, tobacco, and cigarettes is another such reason for the inclusion or exclusion in different social events. Immigrant kids especially face this instability. Most of them feel torn as they have to live two different lives because they originally belonged to one culture that has a set of rules and codes, whereas when you immigrate to a different culture it has a different and often contesting set of rules and codes. Which one do i belong to, and which one do i not is often something that the immigrant kids are challenged with.

i left my country, India, fifteen years ago. i am part of an incredibly small minority of immigrants who actually visit India often. i also qualify for a subset of that small minority who not just visit India but also spend extended lengths of time in India. i must have easily spent 5–6 years, out of my 15 years in the US, in India. i consider myself incredibly fortunate that i am able to do so. But every time i move from one country to another, the people and policies there both make every possible attempt to make me feel that i don't belong.

My friends will invariably take a dig at me or instigate me by making me feel that i have abandoned my country, or constantly remind me how great India is in comparison to the US. They do it innocently and unknowingly, and because they love me but don't have a proper healthy way to communicate their innermost feelings. However, their incapability to communicate makes me feel unwelcome, restricted, and censored. i have limitations on my expressions. i cannot say anything good or nice about the country i am not in. And trust me when i say that both countries have good things and bad things just like every other country and entity in the solar system.

To me it feels like a lifelong ban on expressing my displeasure about anything in India. If some place is stinking and everyone feels it, i still cannot be the first one in the group to point it out because as soon as i do, they all pounce on me with the argument that yes of course you are going to say things to put down our country since you are now all NRI (Non-resident Indian). This instigates me and disturbs me. And i work to absorb the instability instead of radiating it out.

i don't like the unintentional censorship imposed on me by my relatives and friends. "You don't live here anymore, so what do you know of our problems" is something i have often heard. Such behavior pushes me further away from them because even if i give up my life and career in the US and come back, they will still not accept me and let me fully belong.

On the other side, the immigration struggles of the US remind me every minute that i don't belong to this country. My current classification is upgraded from being a "non-resident alien" to a "resident alien." The bottom line is that i am classified as some kind of an alien. An alien is by default someone or something that does not fully belong. How am i expected to belong here with this title? i mean if Superman had so much difficulty in being accepted and belonging then who am i in his comparison. This is also one of the underlying reasons for instability and subsequent radioactivity for the millions of immigrants and migrants and refugees all over the world.

My friend reminded me of yet another mind-boggling aspect of belonging. i had somehow forgotten about it but then while having a conversation, i told him that i am writing about belonging and he reminded and encouraged me that i should mention this for its nuanced uniqueness in stimulating instability. So, believe it or not, the sense of belonging persists even after you die and plays out in the most unimaginable manner. The previous line may not do much justice to what i am going to talk about because it's a bit more complicated than it sounds.

Which ritual and tradition does your body belong to when you are dead? How is the lump of rotting organic matter (your dead body) going to be disposed of is something most people don't give much thought to during most of their lives. But this was a major source of instability in my former girlfriend's life. Which tradition will i belong to after i die. i had never realized that this can even be a thing, but it was. She was convinced that after i die my family will want to dispose my body according to the ritual and tradition of my religion. However, according to her religion if my body was disposed of in any other manner but the one described in that religion, then my soul would not find heaven. And if i didn't go to heaven then she would not be able to unite with me there.

i was flattered (or tormented, couldn't tell at that time) by coming to the realization that this one wanted to be with me even after my death, more importantly in a heaven of her belonging. She would remain upset and stressed about this. i could not even have guessed this in the wildest of my dreams that this could be bothering her. But then as fate had it, forget heaven, we didn't even make it on earth together. To me this was ridiculous because i constantly endeavored to make wherever i lived heavenly, and at the same time my girlfriend was constantly worried about what was going to happen after i die and how would we continue to belong. The radioactivity stemming from the sense of belonging after one's death unbelievably did bring sourness in our relation.

The unanswered "Who do i belong to" as well as the conclusive "who do i belong to" are both sources of different instabilities. In a firm way, i am aware that i belong to my creator, whoever that might be. But till the time i am on earth in this form, this question will continue to perplex me and seven billion others that live at this very moment on the planet. But i can end this reflection by saying that i am very happy because i have clarity on my belonging, and deep appreciation for all my belongings.

Designs—Weird and Unusual

Why do we design difficult things? Many designs are blatantly unusual or weird, say for example the chairs in an airplane or an auditorium. A chair without an armrest is uncomfortable. But a chair where you have to share an armrest with another person and that too a stranger, i'm not only uncomfortable about it but also experience a terrible headache thinking about it. Depending on who sits next to you, you either are relieved or injured for life. For one person with two hands, there should be two armrests. But in most settings, the two armrests you see are only an illusion. You do see two armrests but in fact depending on where you are seated, you either have one or none. The moment you go and sit in one of such chairs, the illusion of the armrests disappears faster than it took to manifest itself. Why bring so much instability and radioactivity in people's lives? And why do people keep accepting and remain silent about such blatant sources of radioactivity?

So, what are some other uncomfortable designs? Bathrooms. I find bathrooms a certain recipe for disaster or in the jargon of this book radioactive explosion due to the lack of standardization and smooth slippery surfaces.

Table 9.1 List of Names of Designs

Names of designs that are weird and unusual
1.
2.
3.
4.
5.
6.
7.
8.
9.
10.

How does one escape it? Don't enter them, which is unfortunately not an option. Most elderly folks fall in a bathroom and invariably break the hip bone or fracture the ball and socket of the hip joint. In most cases this becomes the beginning of their downfall in a real sense. Slippery surfaces for those who have a hard time maintaining balance are bad news. And if they are made to use different bathrooms then the lack of familiarity can lead to an accident. Even if you are familiar, once in a while the probability of an accident to occur is high.

There are many such designs that get the work done but also contribute to the instability of the people using it. What are some designs like the ones mentioned above that you can think of and are sources of instability for the people? (Table 9.1)

The Sensitivity of When to Stop

It is important to stop.... stop thinking, stop doing, stop talking, and even stop being once in a while. To me, it seems like we have just forgotten the existence of a stop switch. i also feel that beyond a certain point there isn't much to gain, or the gains become marginal and, in some cases, simply cease to exist.

Nothing in excess is ever useful. Once you have added the right amount of sugar in the preparation of a cake then adding any more is not going to make it any better. Similarly, if you are by chance able to impress someone there's no need to keep saying more things and risk ruining your impression. i would also say that once you feel like you've lived enough then the need to keep living more is also unnecessary. Similarly, there's no need to keep thinking about something beyond a certain point. Nothing good is going to come from a fixation or an obsession other than instability and radioactivity.

So, it is in one's best interest to realize to stop and more importantly when to stop. There is a critical distinction between stopping and pausing, and one needs to be aware about it. Pausing means a temporary stop and then resuming on the same trajectory, whereas stopping means stopping permanently. Even when it comes to leadership, it is important to know when to stop leading and pass on the baton to someone else. There are not many people that have lived on the planet or are living that can outlive their relevance beyond a certain epoch. Beyond a point if you don't plan to step down, the respect you have earned in the eyes of your followers starts going down.

So, while it is important to develop the sensitivity to stop, it is equally important to know when it is the right time to exit or in other words stop being at a given event or a venue. It is a very important determination that one needs to make pertaining when it is the best time to leave. The old saying, "don't overstay your welcome" was not created for no reason. i am certain that many among your friends that you know are not good at determining their time for exit. While a lot of them don't even know when to show up. But that is a whole different issue. Some are tardy, some are lazy, some are just suffering from apathy, and a whole big bunch from anxiety, social awkwardness, and insecurity about themselves. All these are legit reasons preventing folks from being intuitive and perceptive. So, when is a good time to leave? Well, in many social and cultural circumstances, the timings are fluid, and this is when the determination gets tricky.

i say that when you start feeling alienated by the core group or the host, leave. Don't stop unnecessarily after that. Another hack is when you see the same people and have the same conversation over and over, it's time to go. It's time to go when the pain of staying exceeds the pain of going away. The sensitivity of when to stop doing something or being in some place is a valuable skill to avoid radioactivity.

Contrary to not knowing when to stop is the What next syndrome. No matter what you are doing, you are mentally occupied by what is next. While the previous condition does not allow you to leave the current moment, event, and situation, what next syndrome does not let you live in peace in the current moment, event, and situation.

When a person incessantly needs and wants to keep thinking and wondering about what next then that is a malady. Dissatisfaction with being in the moment or anxiety about what next is problematic. What does the word "next" do to a human? Here is what i think it does:

- One cannot enjoy the moment
- One cannot plan too far
- One cannot focus
- One cannot return information
- Always remain dissatisfied
- Have incomplete and unachieved goals

So, what is that one should do to not think about what next? No, i feel that is not possible, because it is a bit too extreme. And that is an invitation for different radioactivity. Use it one time and get it all out as well as plan and think ahead. But once that dedicated work is done then draw a line and try actively to not spend any time further on it.

Lines and Boundaries

Arbitrary and imagined is a whole lot of our reality. One aspect of our perceived reality that is incredibly seriously drawn and protected is a boundary. Many types of boundaries exist. Boundaries of nations, states, cities, animals and even those that are referred as personal boundaries. One time in my life i was a radio DJ, and i was helping out with a show called Music of India and it's Diaspora. This show would air on WBGUFM which was a student- and community-run radio station of the Bowling Green State University in Ohio, US. At that time, it was all about airway boundaries, the stronger commercial radio stations in Toledo would always breach the boundaries of WBGUFM, which was able to air its shows within a 15-mile radius and this would often be infringed.

Now that the spectrum of lines and boundaries is somewhat clear, it is vital to get into why we expand these constructs to the extent that we forget or choose to ignore our humanity and become willing to argue, fight, or even kill. All this for something arbitrary and imaginary. From an Indian point of view, one of the most toxic lines ever drawn was the line that separated Pakistan from India. The drawing of line and its transformation into a boundary has ignited endless instability and terrible radioactivity. Even after 76 years there is duress and unease among people on both sides. All this because someone imagined that this will be India and that will be Pakistan.

Imaginations are powerful. When we go ahead and ascribe significance to our imaginations, they become our perceived reality. It is rather weird to protect, and even more weird to possess imagined realities. But we don't stop there, we go ahead and develop a corollary system of law and enforcement, courts of law, and even cultivate armies to protect our original imagination of boundaries. Does a human benefit from questioning these imagined realities or even investigating the jingoism affiliated with them? It's a difficult question to answer. But some thought must be devoted to thinking about this because lines and boundaries for the sake of expansion or exploitation or mere existence are generating tremendous radioactivity.

Those who are protecting lines and boundaries are protecting basically just an arbitrarily imagined and greed-inspired thinking of lines on the surface of mother earth. Personal boundaries and relations boundaries are important in keeping your sanity intact. Drawing lines in relations is key to not letting them become toxic. Both the presence and absence of lines and boundaries add instability and radioactivity.

Freedom

Freedom is a tricky concept. It is ultimately desirable because it is believed to be stable. You remain unstable till the time you acquire it. Many nations that were colonized kept fighting for freedom for centuries. And what happened when they finally acquired it? Did the freedom bring a lasting stability with it? I say yes and no because it is pretty complicated. The moment you acquire it feels great. What happens next is not for the faint. My PhD advisor (Dr. Srinivas Melkote) used to say that freedom is a highly contested space. One has to perpetually endeavor and labor to retain it. What i gathered from him and realized was that freedom was a boat with hole in it. The water is perpetually going to keep gushing in. And i have to either keep emptying the boat or not allow the water to come in by plugging the hole. Sometimes you do succeed temporarily in plugging the hole but over time water very well does find a way.

What I was further inspired to question and investigate was who can give freedom away and how do you earn it? Who really has the freedom to give it away upon persuasion or coercion? As a rhetorical question, what would be the cost one would be willing to pay for freedom? We see so many different types of salesmen but have we ever come across a salesman of freedom? On the surface of it, the answer is no. Nobody has ever come across a salesman of freedom. But if you think deeper, you will realize that there are many agents and salesmen of freedom. Now the nature of freedom that is sold is questionable because it is neither everlasting nor guaranteed. Millions of refugees come to the US every year. They come here to enjoy freedom. This has been going on for centuries and it started with a bunch of people who wanted to practice their religion and so they sat in a boat and left for an unknown destination to settle. They escaped instability and settled in stability. Even today hordes of people come to the US from south and central America. They too are escaping the problematic situations in their home countries. Nobody likes to leave their home, their people, their culture, their language, etc. Adverse circumstances and situations compel them to do so. Many of such people encounter salesmen of freedom. They charge you a whole lot of money and assure that they will get you across the border where there is freedom. Car salesmen also sell freedom. They often say to young kids that you can go anywhere you want if you have your own car. You will no longer be dependent on your parents or older siblings. You will be independent. You will be free. Doctors are also salesmen of freedom. They free you from the clutches of pain and illness. They assure you relief and freedom from illness. While no one can give freedom away, there are millions of salesmen of freedom. Isn't that ironic?

Maybe the way i think of freedom here is influenced by ego. It could be my ego seeing and thinking that i or someone is in a position to give freedom away when i don't even have it to give it away then it is nothing but my ego clouding my knowledge. From a viewpoint of ego and in a relational context, i, for argument's sake, think that i give someone the freedom to choose whether they want to be with me or not. The moment i give the opposite person this freedom, an insecurity sneaks in me that what will happen if this person chooses something that i don't want them to or what if they choose something that takes them away from me. Either way, i cannot control their choice. And if i do then i am interfering with the flow. Trust, faith, and lots of looking at the universe for true compassion is what is needed. The cosmos is your best companion and will keep working for you to send you the best vibration match. And if that is not available then it is you, just you.

True freedom can neither be granted nor be gained. True freedom is not the freedom of the body. True freedom is the freedom of the mind. My mind cannot be freed because it is already free. Now wait. You have to ask yourself, is my mind free or is it reined and restricted and blocked? In theory, its abilities are infinite, its horizons are endless but the state and form in which you exist is just one of the countless possibilities. This is the one single reality that has succeeded or stumbled and managed to manifest itself. This could be an example of manifesting and exercising freedom. Only one reality but multiple possibilities. What about the existence of multiple realities? i don't think so. This is where non-duality comes into play. But then what is this whole fascination with fantasy or the fantasizing with what if? Now that could be an illusion or an old feud with evolution. Let's explore both the possibilities and see where they lead us.

Possibility 1: the whole fantasizing of what if it is an illusion.

It could very well be true. But then the Bhagwad Gita goes to the level where Lord Krishna says that.**

**The above portion on freedom remained incomplete because while i was sitting and writing this portion two of my friends interrupted me and disturbed me. i had then hoped that i could pick up from where i had left it and finish it and despite trying several times, i am unable to go back to my line of thought. i hope that you can finish this portion with your own personal twist. You are free to do so. *

Flow

This word has me and my fascination ensnared. And when ensnared by such a mighty concept, it takes a while to rescue yourself. You might even need backup and call in for reinforcements. Unfortunately, i still haven't earned my Avengers membership, so no backup for me. And therefore, i don't think i am at a stage where I can proclaim to be completely free of the snare. Thus, i will share with you here, the little progress that i have made so far without the Avengers.

Flow is within us and outside of us. Flow is what surrounds us and abounds us. There are countless types and forms of flows in our vicinity as well as in the larger ecosystem. The trap here is that as soon as you get sensitized with this concept, you start seeing it everywhere. And then there is no escape. Wherever you go, you see a flow. It follows you more persistently than a shadow. A shadow, at least, disappears in the absence of light. Flow does not. The snare further tightens as you see it everywhere but don't understand it well enough and that is when you just get sucked in the vortex of your thoughts. Once you get sucked in, it is incredibly difficult to resurface.

One of the first contexts that occurred to me when i started thinking about flow was of a river flowing. After that the second thought was of animals and birds in large quantities migrating across countries and continents. The great migration in Africa where hundreds of thousands of animals flow from dried up torrid regions to greener pastures. Then came to my mind the expression "flow of thought." Breeze, flow of traffic (which nowadays is incessant), blood flow, supply chain and flow of logistics, etc. So many flows around us and within us. i want to demonstrate the tightening of the trap by giving you an example of where my mind went just with the first flow, the flowing of a river. i will circle back and meet you on the other end to take this further. Enjoy flowing for a short while.

High up on a mighty mountain, hidden in plain sight, behind a translucent veil of colossal clouds, is the origin of a flow. The mighty mountain is constantly engaged in a tug-of-war with the colossal clouds, and when it does overpower the colossal clouds, as a reward for its victory, it gets to tower above them to glance at the sun. To honor the victory, the sun too, sort of, obliges and glances back. A sidelong glance from the sun is enough to melt the mightiest of the mountains.

The melting of the mighty mountain creates timid and bashful droplets. These droplets present themselves reluctantly at first. The reluctance is obvious because as soon as the droplet drips, it ceases being the mighty mountain. Unsure whether it wants to remain the mighty mountain or be the vulnerable droplet, it aptly displays apprehension for initiating its crushing descent all by itself. This separation is understandably the most difficult. But by now you have already guessed what the droplet eventually decides to do.

It dives headfirst. As soon as it does so another one replaces it and is ready to repeat the crushing feat. Droplet after droplet drips and this is the origin of a flow. The mighty mountain unbeknownst to the drop has already provided it the boost to succeed in the form of its steep slope. The droplet which is now together with countless more is again no more a droplet. It is a stream, and it flows. Twisting and turning it meets more of its kind gathering force. At times the flow also falls from great heights, and we awe at these droplets falling. Hordes of people spend hours of time and energy so that they can marvel at the courage of innumerable timid droplets that are about to jump and transform into mesmerizing waterfalls. Just like a baby learning to walk falls many a times, the stream, which may now be a little river falls often, our timid droplet also falls often while merging with more and more of its kind. Junctions where different flows meet are holy.

We gather at these junctions where flows meet to pay our respects and revere the new creation. With the combined forces, the flow becomes stronger and becomes an enormous river, no more hidden or quiet. Thunderous and crushing, this river has become. Thousands gather at its bank and pay their respect and in exchange expect the flow to wash them off of their impurities. The gushing flow of a river flows by many miles to meet with the sea where once again it ceases to be sweet and refreshing and instead transforms itself into brackish and salty. As you very well know the journey of flow does not end here. The journey of the flow is eternal.

This is just one example of a vortex that you can potentially get sucked into. There are many more. Another flow is of new viruses that we have seen in the last ten years. Almost every year there has been a new virus that wreaked havoc on one or the other part of earth. The most recent (COVID-19) brought the world to a halt and emerging from it is not going to be easy. i do wonder what type of deadly or godly virus will the flow bring next.

To not end my musing and to flow with it a little longer, i had come up with a philosophy some five years ago about flow, which you must read. When i shared it with my mother, she instantly told me, "Arpan, don't be an idiot." That should tell you how awesome that philosophy must be. If you ask me, it is. My philosophy is a one-way ticket away from instability and radioactivity to peace and even flourishing. So here goes.

There is an invisible flow of give and take that happens perennially in an individual's life. There are people, situations, and circumstances that exist around you only and only to give to you. They give you love, warmth, security, comfort, etc. Contrary to that there are people, situations, and circumstances that exist around you only and only to take from you. They take from you your peace of mind, stability, happiness, prosperity, fame, etc. This is a flow which an individual should not try to disrupt.

If someone is taking from you let him/her take it. Don't resist. If someone is giving to you take it. Don't fight it. By resisting either, you disturb not just the flow but also your inner peace and stability. One has to work hard on oneself to ensure that one doesn't disrupt the flow or disturb your inner stability. If you are able to achieve this, irrespective of what happens, you remain unperturbed. i have tried this, and I can proudly say to you that do try this at home. Do it gradually and increase it incrementally. It's a way to balance your inner yin and yang.

According to my theory of Flow, your stability hinges tremendously on your indifference. You invite instability when you don't graciously give to the one who exists to take. A child born with a congenital disease, or a grown-up teen gets into an accident and becomes physically disabled. This child becomes a taker due to his or her doing or the doing of destiny. This child is going to take a lot of things away from the parents. Now if the parents resist this then they are going to go through immense agony. Since this example is about a child, there is still a high willingness to give but imagine if a thief or a burglar comes and asks for your money, watch, mobile, etc. Problem happens when we don't give it all graciously. This is when the propensity of the thief or the burglar to become violent. A tire gets punctured to make you delayed and destroy your peace and stability in the moment. If you resist it and don't handle the situation gracefully then the situation will surely worsen, and you will not feel like you. Donate the time that the puncture has asked for without agonizing over it. If you don't give, you are the one becoming radioactive, the punctured tire is not going to feel a thing.

Opposite to what is stated above, there are some people who only exist to give and when we don't take from them without doubt it again brings us instability. When someone gives us for no reason we often doubt. Our ancestors and experiences have taught us to not take from anyone who gives for no reason as there is always an ulterior motive. Now that is certainly true that there are multiple people who have malintentions but because of them one cannot doubt or blame everyone. When your relatives or cousins do something nice or kind, don't doubt them just accept what they are doing and embrace them. If you down the rabbit hole that this person may want something for me and that is why he or she must be doing something nice or in other words, the rabbit hole of doubting then you will not be able to enjoy the gift or remain at peace.

Hence, i say that become cognizant of the Flow around you and be extra mindful to not disrupt it. Flow is all around and inside you. Don't disrupt either. The flow of blood and other chemicals is so important. Due to your habits and lifestyle, you actively work towards disrupting it. Once disrupted, all the joys and fun out of your life is gone. Sometimes even life is gone. There is no stopping you once you go with the flow. You remain forever stable and still. And eventually flourish despite good or bad. Some people only flourish when things are good. They are not one with the flow. A flourishing person flourishes despite everything. This, probably, is also the reason why we don't like to say goodbye and in my humble opinion will never perfect it as well because no one likes to disrupt the flow. Hope you have enjoyed my flow. Hence, i thank you and wish you good flows onto the next chapter on Creative Psyche.

10

CREATIVE PSYCHE

A rehaul or a rewiring of existing psyche for its transformation to a more creative and flexible psyche is paramount. i would like to highlight how Creativity must be used as a tool to break the deep conditionings of the human mind and bring about the right psyche or mindset to be able to absorb radioactivity instead of exploding every time when there is instability. A creative mindset is critical to ensuring absorption-based sustenance instead of an explosion-based sustenance.

Human sustenance is currently hinged on being heavily explosion-based. i say this with lot of sadness because such sustenance is the seed of all that is dark and devilish. All the violent and non-violent conflicts among humankind and the thoughtless rampage of human nature is coming from an explosion-based sustenance. See what is happening in Ukraine and Russia. See what happening in Israel, Palestine, Lebanon, and Iran. It is all an exclusive display of explosion-based sustenance.

i often ask myself this question, what is the need to pluck a flower? Why would anyone want to pluck a flower? Are either the need or the greed really justified? i honestly don't think so. There are many forms of deep-rooted instabilities within us and unless we actively endeavor to eliminate them, we will continue to drown ourselves in conflict with no resolution or a creative solution to any.

My singular hope for humanity is that we never cross the threshold where we are beyond reconciliation. If a problem exists or arises at a supposed mindset level then to overcome that problem, an individual has to alter his or her mindset and make it bigger and better. Without an incremental change in the extant mindset or the knowledge level, it is practically impossible to solve any problem. If you are unable to push a punctured car for more than

DOI: 10.4324/9781032627564-10

20 meters, unless you work on changing your strength or in other words making yourself stronger, you are not going to be able to move it any more than 20 meters. The same goes for instability, the only way any instability can be minimized and absorbed is through a change in the mindset or the psyche.

The constant ability to grow larger and alter the perspective is possible only through creative flexibility. Enlightenment is another way to achieve the same but not everyone can achieve that and once you do achieve it, you are permanently sorted. So, what can the people who cannot achieve enlightenment or are destined to achieve it do as a way to counter instability by absorbing it and not shirking from it? They have to exclusively rely on creativity.

Creativity is defined in many ways as many things but at the core of it all, it is the ability to entertain "Mithya." Mithya is anything and everything that does not have to ability to remain constant or unchanged when passing through time. Everything that is changing, fleeting, and ephemeral is Mithya. And our creative abilities and proclivities are also Mithya themselves because they too change with time. Children are considered to be extremely creative but as they grow their creativity diminishes. Those who work on it, for them creativity may enhance as well. Our body is Mithya since it is constantly changing. It is therefore said that we are not our bodies but we know nothing other than our body and so we develop this obsessive infatuation with it and misunderstand it as our own selves. This is nothing but ignorance. Mithya is flexible and can change its scope and influence.

In the enlightened state there is no scope for creativity. Creativity is a staple for ones still frolicking in and concerned about Mithya. For example, an apple is a Mithya because with time it changes its form, taste, and texture and ultimately even perishes. All the different manifestations of apple, which are differing in shape, size, taste, color, and aroma, are all real. Yet they are all temporary and fleeting. Such transferences are the creative flexibility and stretching of the Mithya. The example of an apple is relatively easy to understand but these constructs do not remain as easy to grasp when applied to most other aspects of our personal lives such as identity, relations, possessions, acquisitions, and declarations. Everything we hold so dear is nothing but Mithya.

To give another quick example, it is easy to be around our beloved partner or members of our family. But when suffering from a sickness the very same beloved one exhibits a different nature. They could be more needy or clingy and even thankless and overbearing. Suddenly the same person who we want to be around and near all the time, becomes very hard to be around or near. i can give two examples from my life.

While i am narrating my experience, this is something that a large majority of doctoral students experience. The reason they feel hurt is because they have not yet enlarged their creative psyche and developed the ability to see things in a proper perspective. They continue to see things in a narrow perspective. All Ph.D. students have to go through their verbal defense of their research. They have to present to a committee of experts how they have discovered new knowledge. This knowledge could be exploratory in nature or confirmatory in nature. The committee's responsibility is to ensure that you have learned the fundamentals of discovering new knowledge and whether you have shown sufficient evidence for them to give you the diploma that grants you the credibility to be an independent researcher.

In the process, all your committee members ask you questions, usually tough ones. The committee is made up of an external member, other professors, and the chair of the committee who is your guide and advisor. Your advisor is normally the person with whom you have been through several thick and thin situations. This person knows the ins and outs of your dissertation and is your biggest cheerleader and champion in the entire process. Bear in mind that I am giving this example to explain mithya to you. During the time of my dissertation defense, the most difficult question came to me from my advisor. In that moment you feel uncertain and confused. You also feel cheated and betrayed because suddenly the person who is supposed to be on your side is not on your side. This is a debilitating feeling. You keep asking yourself why did the person change. Was this person never on your side or what? All this is due to our narrow existence with a limited creative psyche.

Your advisor is still your advisor and still your champion and cheerleader but that does not mean that the advisor should not discharge his or her righteous duty. The issue here is not with the advisor. It is in your obfuscated understanding that just because someone is on your side they will behave as you expect them to behave. This unexpected change in emotions and feelings makes you unstable.

Creativity is required for mental flexibility and realization that any source of instability is also Mithya. i say so because nothing can bother us or rattle us constantly all the time. The severity of botheration changes from time to time. You might argue that many sources of instability do not allow us to even sleep. That's true. But when you do sleep the source of agony is forgotten. It is likely that the next day the agony and the agony-inspired instability increases but then it is also possible that the next day it can decrease or entirely disappear. The first and most important lesson about creative rehauling of the brain is the realization that the source of instability and the instability itself are all part of the Mithya. In other words, time will act on it and that will alter or entirely eliminate the instability.

The realization that any instability is fleeting or temporary is the first step in creatively rewiring oneself to be able to absorb the instability. Absorbing instability means nullifying the ability of the instability to stimulate dissonance and disharmony in you. In every automobile there are shock absorbers. Every automobile maker is aware that once the automobile is on the road there will be bumps and jumps. If these inevitable destabilizers exist, then their presence will harm the automobile by damaging the integrity of the vehicle through enhanced wear and tear. In addition, they will also ensure that the passenger that is seated in the automobile does not enjoy the ride because it is not smooth, and the shocks are intense.

We have the same issue with our life. The road of life is full of bumps and jumps, and in addition unexpected turns and meanderings as well as bad weather conditions brought in by relational turbulences impact. All these challenge our structural integrity. But where are our shock absorbers? We do have them. But then why do we never explicitly speak about them or teach others to use them. i reflected upon this and realized that while growing up my family has shared with me and taught me through living their life with four shock absorbers. These four shock absorbers help us substantially to absorb the instability and reduce its impact on us.

The Four Shock Absorbers

The four shock absorbers require creative rewiring of the brain. The four are listed here in a vernacular language of India called Gujarati, which is my mother tongue. They are Ashe, Gamshe, Chalshe, and Favshe. These are highly sophisticated shock absorbers. Until we reach the technological advances where the car of our life travels suspended in air using magnetic force where the journey is smooth, it is important that we use these four. Even we if get to the magnetic force level or the flying in the air level, there are still chances of air turbulences and braking mechanism failure. So, the possibility of instability persists everywhere because at the end of it this is all Mithya.

Ashe

Ashe is the ultimate shock absorber. It translates to "its ok" or "it's alright" or "it's fine" or "so be it." Ashe instantly inundates you with the ability to forgive and accept. You go to a restaurant and get the wrong food delivered, you say Ashe and the agony of being served wrong food disappears. Anyone comes and tells you that this person is scheming against you and wants to do you harm. You say Ashe and then person will never return to inform you anything poisonous. Ashe is the unwarranted acceptance that bypasses many of your otherwise active reactances and resistances. It is immediate and effective. Ashe also comes from a place of content and satisfaction. More importantly it also comes from a place of large hearted magnanimity.

Chalshe

Chalshe is an attitudinal shock absorber. "it'll work" or "this'll do" is the translation of it. Chalshe is about the simplistic and minimalist attitude. Acceptance for whatever is the least possible requirement is the Chalshe magic. Making this decision is often referred to as compromising or settling for less. But having this shock absorber gives an individual a tremendous edge. Especially if you are a guest, having this in your arsenal will reduce so much instability at your end as well as for the host. Hosts these days are very anxious. The art and habit of hosting is rapidly getting lost and hence hosting is becoming something to stress over and be anxious about rather than being joyful and delightful about. Any guest who can say Chalshe automatically becomes a sanyasi or even better a Vairagi. A vairagi is a person who does not have any unnecessary affinity towards or against anything or anyone. A vairagi is a dispassionate individual embracing of all and the word Chalshe is often at the very tip of his attitudinal tongue. Bear in mind that we are all guests on planet earth. We remain guests here only for a hundred or so years. And if we learn to say Chalshe to our host, our mother earth and our life, we will be such amazing guests and our lives too will be blissful.

Chalshe is an explicative that indicates an absence of strong preference. Madam we have the "dupatta" only in this color. That will work. This represents that the person is seeing the dupatta for its core utility and value, and not its additional aesthetic sense or appeal. Sir, we don't have the latest smartphone model that you want in xyz color, but we do have it in this generic color. Chalshe. This will work. i'll not delay my purchase decision and instead buy it. Chalshe is a shock absorber that prevents attitudinal misery and instability stemming from choices and preferences. While Chalshe is a shock absorber, it is not airtight. This is because not everyone is able to fully imbibe the Chalshe mentality. While once or twice out of politeness you may make it work but then once the quota of politeness is depleted boundaries start being drawn and being adhered to. Chalshe also leaves some room for envy. Also this might work differently in group situations. If you are traveling with a group on an organized tour. And twice all the other tourists get an air-conditioned room, but you don't. You Chalshe it, and you are ok with it and will make it work but if this becomes a habit then you will mildly revolt. However, if the other tourists have paid more for air-conditioned facilities, then you can also be envious of them (Figure 10.1).

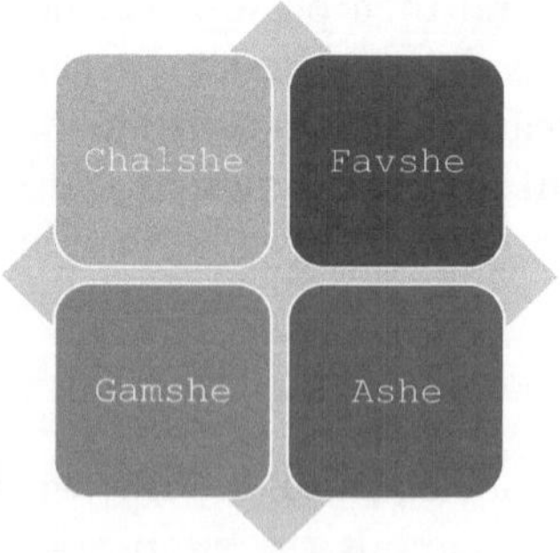

FIGURE 10.1 The Four Shock Absorbers.

Gamshe

Gamshe is the shock absorber of acceptance. Liking is the first and a major step of accepting a situation or a person. Gamshe translates to "I'll like it" or "likeable." Anything that is likeable is eventually also acceptable. What you like, you often tend to enjoy. This is also a creative requirement of the brain where the brain is being overridden by your executive authority that you like something, and this forces the brain to reduce reactance and instead fall in line. The Gamshe shock absorber creates an alternative narrative in the head with the hope of making it the dominant narrative, eventually reducing or even eliminating any instability emerging from it.

Favshe

Favshe translates to "i'll adjust" or "i will accommodate." Favshe serves as a shock absorber at the behavioral level. Behavioral adjustment and accommodation of a potential source of instability is not easy but relatively manageable when it comes to it. To adjust is to require one to be flexible and open to potential future attacks of instability. After living in a country that affords you lots of space for more than a dozen years and coming from a group that has been afforded privileged and special status for certain days in a year where at least in the past people would go out of their way to not come near you for risking touching you, i tried to deploy the Favshe shock absorber at a temple. Temples in India, especially in South or that is where the trend started and now it may be a pan-India thing, have multiple lines leading you to the place where you can stand and do the darshan of the deity of the temple. The special line or the VIP line will require you to pay a certain amount of money. Paying the money and going through the VIP line cuts short the number of people between you and the deity by geometric progressions. This greatly reduces instability.

My instability in temples comes from random and unknown people touching me or standing unnecessarily close to me. i don't like to do the darshan or pray when there are people standing very close to me or touching me. It ruins my internal stability and i am unable to concentrate or focus on my prayer. It ruins the vibe and i have left many a times from temples or even religious rituals because there are too many people who want to take the benefit of partaking in religious rituals and don't mind piling on one another.

Once i decided that i will use the Favshe shock absorber and did not opt for the VIP line. All was well for the most part of it but then things started going south once we got closer to the deity. The desperation of the people behind me grew many folds and they kept pushing me from behind. Since i had the shock absorber the instability from it did not bother me too much. But i still had to tell them to keep a decent distance so that they as well as i can enjoy the darshan.

And no disrespect is meant here but the elderly women in such spaces are a menace. They are pushy, impatient, demanding, and just don't want to listen to anything that comes out of a human mouth. It does not matter to them if the human mouth is mine or the temple authorities or the police in the temple. They are at their peak levels of assertion. While i was able to do darshan but i did not enjoy the darshan much because of the excessive touching and pushing. i also understand their side of the issue that they are all relatively short. They are all mostly in the range of 5-5.5″ tall. And most likely there will be someone taller in front of them blocking their view. And if someone 6 ft. tall like me is standing then they will absolutely not be able to see the deity. They have my sympathy and empathy. i mostly let shorter people go in front of me so that they can see the deity and so can i. But it does not work that way and that is the time I have to deploy Favshe.

Santosh-Satisfaction/Contentment

Santosh or Satisfaction or Contentment is ten times more potent than the four shock absorbers. Dissatisfaction with what you have and are as opposed to what you want in any and all spheres of life is a perpetually pestering source of instability making a large subset of humanity radioactive.

There are no limits to the wants and desires of a human. If a person has a small home, then they will want a big home, if he has one car then he will want four cars, if he has one company then he will want more companies. Everyone keeps wanting more. When they don't get it, and most people don't get what they want, they become unstable. Actually, it is not an exaggeration to say that nobody gets enough of what they want. This makes people so unstable and radioactive. Moreover, to get and acquire all that you need to acquire is also not the end of instability and radioactivity. The issue is not with acquiring or not acquiring. It's the absence of satisfaction in both the states. i will give the example of an uncle of mine here. i deeply respect and adore this uncle of mine. He is endearing, committed, and keeps the family together. In his younger days, he met a girl and fell in love with her. This was still a teenage crush sort of thing and not much could be done about it since the girl and her family moved to a different city. Years passed by and the young boy was now a young man. He accidentally ran into the same girl in a different city where he was studying. He found out that the girl too was living there. They were both madly in love with one another. The young man did some dangerous things like riding on the outside of a train to get to this girl's Bharatnatyam performance in a different city. He did not have money to buy a ticket and risked getting into the train without a ticket. When he saw the ticket collector, he panicked and went to the spot where two coaches were connected and snuck out and remained hanging in a moving train. Anyhow they were able to finally convince their parents and got married to be with one another for a long matrimony. You can say that the boy finally got what he wanted. The boy did get what he wanted until he realized that the girl's health is a bit fragile, and she does not show much proactivity in keeping herself fit and fine. She is lethargic when it comes to giving her health a priority. This became the bane of their existence where he would try to encourage her to take better care and she would not but then when things happened, he would obviously be there for her wholeheartedly. He did not have a problem being there for her, he had a problem with seeing her in an unhealthy state because after all she was the love of his life. While he got what he wanted but he still did not get what he wanted in totality, and he always regretted it.

Satisfaction is an extremely tricky thing. You cannot get satisfaction by acquiring something or achieving something. The satisfaction you get there is temporary and nothing but an instigator for going after more. Dissatisfaction is a state of mind which you can have despite having, acquiring, or achieving something and satisfaction is state of mind which you can possess without any actual achievements or acquisitions. Satisfaction is the end of desire, greed, obsessions, ambitions, longings, and more.

Also noteworthy is that there is not really any satisfaction in more. After you have eaten and satiated your hunger, if someone offers you more you will reject it. In many restaurants, they give us mouth-freshening mints after our dinner. Often it happens that some of it gets stuck in the molars and premolars. Until and unless all that is stuck is cleaned off, a person is restless. Satisfaction emerging from consumption and acquiring is short-lived and fragile. A little more or a little less of it and your happiness is still disrupted. I once again repeat that you cannot be satisfied by acquiring or achieving anything. Satisfaction comes from the knowledge of the true self and a constant connection with it. Cultivating this is the cultivation of a Creative Psyche. It's an expansive psyche that absorbs everything. Through a Creative Psyche, turbulence of change can become fertile ground for new ideas and solutions, provided we approach it with a mindset that embraces possibility rather than fear. Rather than viewing instability as a threat, we can see it as an invitation to explore new dimensions of our capabilities.

The Alchemy of Absorption versus Explosion

Creative Psyche has the incredible ability to absorb instability and bring about stability. An unstable person is prone to radioactive explosions and a stable human will absorb the radioactivity instead. The metaphorical and symbolic representations of the two responses an individual can have, are worth exploring here further keeping in mind the role of Creative Psyche. Absorption as opposed to explosion captures the essence of how different mindsets handle instability. In this book, i argue that a creative psyche excels in absorption, by seamlessly integrating challenges and destabilizing agents into the fabric of a normal human's existence. In contrast, an uncreative psyche or a rigid mindset may react explosively or discriminatorily by struggling to cope with the demands of change or expansion in cognition and invariably becoming overwhelmed by stress. Stress is one of the most common explicit manifestations of internal instability.

Bear in mind that instability is always on the inside and in the mind of an individual. Now there might be several external stimulants of instability around us but the thing to remember here is that they don't all bother us or make us unstable. Moreover, they also don't matter to us equally. Every day thousands of car accidents occur. Not one of them irks us. But supposedly one day, only one accident happens on the entire planet and that involves our loved one, then it will bother us and make us unstable. If you come to think of it, then we are already immune to the effects of accidents but when it happens to someone that we are close to, the shield of immunity becomes ineffective. I can give another example to further explain this. Every year millions of students somewhere on the planet fail in their exams. Alternatively, every year many students also excel in their exams. This does not make us happy or unhappy. But when your child is in a school and if he or she fails or excels then depending on the outcome, you will be either greatly happy or inconsolably sad. My point here is that the presence of the Creative Psyche is a default. It is the superimposition of human affection, attachment, and emotions that make things further complicated. In adverse conditions and in favorable conditions, if one can observe a standard neutrality, then it can be said that a creative psyche preexists but under certain circumstances, which is often for many they do not come in handy. Absorption versus Explosion for those who have made it until here in the book is a mere choice. For those who do not have such exposure, it is still a reaction. A reaction that is subjective and emerging from ignorance.

In a world out there, a radioactive explosion in reaction to instability often involves anger, aggression, irritation, stress, resistance, and an overall sense of being overwhelmed. Such a state of being is characterized by a struggle to maintain control, leading to emotional and psychological upheaval. Fear of the unknown future, as explained in the anxiety chapter is single handedly one of the biggest contributors to radioactive explosions. Once this fear enters into an individual's system, then it fights aggressively to take over the realms of that individual's thoughts, actions, and decisions. And if a destabilizing instance occurs, depending on its intensity, it can hinder our ability in the moment to detach, adapt and grow, trapping us in a cycle of anxiety and frustration. This is damaging not only to the person but also to the people surrounding the person. The caveat here is that a radioactive explosion or an outburst can be helpful to the person since it rids him or her of the instability. A person cuts you in traffic, you get mad first and then yell and abuse that person and you feel better. But if you had to just suck it up without the chance of letting it out or giving it back, that is when instability persists and stays with you. This can reduce with time or even get aggravated with time. Ultimately, a person's deep desire to be stable will somehow find a way for the person to angrily lash out at someone weaker to him or her.

Many might argue here that what about controlled explosions or outbursts. This happens regularly in areas of high snowfalls. Places where there is a danger of avalanche blocking the highways, especially in arboreal Canada and other arctic regions, they do controlled explosions and artificial avalanches, which are smaller in intensity and not as damaging. They are manageable due to their less intense size and nature. Well, you can go and workout or play a racquet game with high intensity and get rid of the instability. If you need to get rid of pent-up anger, squash is the best. You actually need to hit that ball hard. The Squash ball is so made that it absorbs the power and changes in shape ultimately not resulting in bouncing at all. Go try it and see how your old anger is released or not.

In the realm of absorption, instability is absorbed into the psyche as a source of learning and growth. This mindset transforms challenges into opportunities, viewing each obstacle as a chance to adapt, innovate, and evolve. It involves a proactive approach to change, where we actively seek to understand and integrate new experiences into our lives. Absorption is the characteristic of a mature being. A mature being is like an ocean. While many things get emptied in it, the sea level does not waver. It welcomes everything without being perturbed. If you have four cars and have a garage large enough to accommodate ten cars, then the addition of two or three more cars is not going to be a problem. If you have a five-bedroom home, and there are eight guests coming then you can easily accommodate two in each in four rooms. Similarly, if you have space in your being then much of the unstability coming your way will be easily accommodated or absorbed without an issue. When you are sixty years old, the bursting of your balloon will not rattle you as much as it did when you were six. To feel the same detachment with things in your personal life is a sign of maturity. Such maturity needs to be cultivated in all the dealings and aspects of lives. That's called working on the absorptive ability.

i say it's an ability because not everyone is able to discharge it equally. We all have different appetites for absorbing profit and loss. In reality, we have infinite ability to absorb both but due to the prevailing ignorance about our own abilities and our attachments to the ephemeral and illusory materials and society, our absorptive ability becomes greatly restricted. This also means that it can be developed and enhanced. One can work on it and make it infinitely expansive. Through knowledge and clarity about the core essentials it is possible to enhance absorptive abilities. Creative Psyche will be a stepping stone to cultivating and developing such clarity and knowledge.

Cultivating the Creative Psyche

Here in this section, i supply a few different preliminary ways to cultivate Creative Psyche. They touch upon some of the essential aspects, which need to change in human cognition and comprehension.

Opening the Mind: The Art of Openness

Openness is the cornerstone of a creative psyche. It involves embracing new experiences, ideas, and perspectives with curiosity and receptivity. It assumes a non-skewed approach and a non-biased approach to everything. Openness is about not allowing knee-jerk judgments or preconceived notions to cloud or meddle with your interaction. To foster openness, you must engage in novel experiences. Deliberately seek out experiences that challenge your comfort zone. Going beyond the comfort zone offers a unique reward. To do so you can also foster new connections and collaborations. Collaborate with others to gain diverse perspectives and ideas. Teamwork can enhance creativity and lead to more innovative solutions. Collaborating with others brings different viewpoints and expertise to the problem-solving process. Moreover, going outside of your comfort zone could be as simple as exploring a new hobby, traveling to unfamiliar places, or engaging in conversations with diverse individuals. Each new experience offers a chance to expand your horizons and stimulate creative thinking. If you can't think of anything my suggestion will be to start with Sudoku. It is a lot of fun and by the way does not involve math. To solve a Sudoku puzzle you don't need to solve any mathematical equation.

Another thing you can do is to practice reflective inquiry. Cultivate the habit of asking questions and exploring different viewpoints. Reflect on your assumptions and beliefs. Be open to reevaluating them in light of new information. i spoke about some of this in an earlier chapter on beliefs as well as biases. It's refreshing to step out of these and see the world in a different light. Reflective inquiry encourages deeper understanding and fosters a mindset of continuous learning. Another suggestion for engaging in openness is to engage in mindfulness practices to increase self-awareness and foster a non-judgmental attitude toward new experiences. Mindfulness can help you stay present and open to the richness of the moment, enhancing your ability to embrace and integrate new ideas. There are countless videos and tutorials on mindfulness on YouTube that you can watch and practice along. One thing that i would suggest is to watch the walking videos. What more do you see when someone else is doing the walking and you are just mindfully seeing and engaging with the noise and views. Try to see the many things that you would otherwise miss when you are yourself walking.

Embracing Flexibility: The Dance of Adaptability

Flexibility is a key attribute of the creative psyche, enabling individuals to adapt to changing circumstances and modify their approaches as needed. Flexibility of the mind is one of the biggest strengths when it comes to cultivating absorptive abilities. Flexibility and adaptability enable you to accommodate so much more with such relative ease that you will positively surprise your own self.

The first thing to do here is to challenge your default convergent thinking patterns. Identify and question fixed patterns or assumptions that may be limiting your ability to adapt or be flexible. Consider alternative perspectives and be open to revising your views. Challenging fixed patterns and assumptions can help you break free from rigid thinking and embrace new possibilities. Another must do thing is to experiment with new approaches. The key word here is approaches. Your approach has to be new and be experimented with. Regularly experiment with new methods, strategies, or ways of thinking. Embrace experimentation of new approaches as a natural part of the process to cultivate your Creative Psyche. Experimentation allows you to explore different avenues and discover innovative solutions. Experiment with using your non-dominant hand for a day for every major thing that you have to do. Try a different route to get to your office. Try looking at a map upside down and figuring out your route. We are so used to seeing north side up. Instead try seeing a different direction up and make sense of things there. You can also start including another aspect of generating multiple solutions. When talking about approaches, approach problems with the mindset of generating multiple potential solutions. Explore various options and consider their potential impacts. Generating multiple solutions allows you to evaluate different approaches and choose the most effective one.

The ultimate Tango move in the dance of flexibility is to adapt to uncertainty. Practice accepting uncertainty as an inherent aspect of life. Uncertainty offers an opportunity of ambiguity and poesis, which are both major assets when it comes to Creative Psyche. Poesis is the ability to create something out of nothing, which often comes in handy in situations when there is great uncertainty. You can also develop strategies for managing uncertainty, such as setting flexible goals and maintaining a positive outlook. Adapting to uncertainty involves embracing the unknown and viewing it as an opportunity for growth. This is once again where Poesis and creativity are extremely helpful. Engage in continuous learning to stay adaptable and open to new ideas. This includes formal education, self-study, or skill development. Lifelong learning helps you stay relevant and responsive to changing circumstances. In addition, allow your goals and plans to evolve based on new information and changing circumstances. Flexibility can enhance your ability to respond to change effectively. Adjusting your goals ensures that they remain relevant and achievable.

Building Resilience: The Strength to Bounce Back

Resilience is the capacity to recover from setbacks and maintain a positive outlook despite challenges. This is something you will need in the beginning. Later on, you will not need this because there will be no setbacks or a need to recover. For initially building resilience you can start with prioritizing self-care. Engage in self-care practices that support your mental, emotional, and physical well-being. This includes maintaining a balanced lifestyle, managing stress, and seeking support when needed. Self-care helps you build the strength to face challenges with resilience. Do not ignore sleep. Neglecting sleep is the biggest enemy of self-care. Do know that sleep is not a passive activity or a waste of time. It is an active time very much needed for superior functioning of the brain. So please do sleep well.

Adopt a Growth Mindset. Embrace a growth mindset that views challenges as opportunities for learning and development. Focus on progress and improvement rather than perfection. A growth mindset encourages you to see setbacks as valuable learning experiences. Another thing you can do is to reflect on your achievements. Don't dwell on them or remain stuck to them or make them all that you have had to offer to the world. But do regularly reflect on past successes and achievements. Use these reflections as a source of motivation and confidence in your ability to overcome future challenges. Reflecting on achievements helps you recognize your strengths and build resilience. These can be as simple as a time when you made a few people laugh or when you did not plan to help but ended up helping somebody.

Nurturing Curiosity: The Spark of Discovery

Curiosity is a driving force behind creativity and innovation. Curiosity to learn and know must be cultivated. Curiosity is the prime characteristic of a learner. To nurture curiosity, ask questions, and lots of them. Cultivate a habit of asking questions and seeking answers. Approach problems with a sense of wonder and a desire to explore. The sense of wonderment is a wonderful experience, enabling fascination instead of frustration. Asking questions helps you uncover new insights and stimulates creative thinking. Dynamism in the space and place also stimulates creativity. Design a home or a workspace that encourages creativity and experimentation. This may involve creating spaces and opportunities for natural brainstorming, collaboration, and risk-taking. A stimulating environment fosters innovation and creative thinking.

i will also recommend that you explore diverse interests. Engage with a variety of subjects and interests. Exposure to different fields can stimulate new ideas and insights. Exploring diverse interests allows you to make connections between seemingly unrelated areas. One way I do this is by going to a library and randomly picking up a book and then reading it. I may not read the entire book, but it still takes me to an entirely unknown land of knowledge, and this further sparks my curiosity and my desire to make connections between different otherwise unconnected concepts and realms. What this does is that it also encourages playful exploration. And i say that allow yourself time for creative play and experimentation. Engage in activities that stimulate your imagination and foster a sense of discovery. Incorporate creative thinking into problem-solving and decision-making processes. Align creativity with practical considerations to develop effective and novel solutions. Integrating creativity into processes ensures that innovative ideas are explored effectively. Playful exploration encourages you to approach challenges with a sense of curiosity and creativity.

These are some ways in which you can slowly and surely expand and cultivate your Creative Psyche. In doing so you will also encounter some resistance and challenges. One needs to be mindful of how our mind resists change and the expansion and cultivation of the Creative Psyche. Hence it is critical to navigate the barriers and overcome them. First and foremost, Acknowledge and Address Fear that lives in and through you. Recognize and address any fears or anxieties related to change. Seek support or guidance if needed to manage these fears. Addressing fear helps you confront and overcome resistance to change. The next thing to do is to set achievable goals in a given timeline. Break down larger changes into smaller, manageable steps. This can make the process of expanding and cultivating your Creative psyche less overwhelming and more achievable. Setting achievable goals helps you make gradual progress and build confidence. From time to time do celebrate progress. Acknowledge and celebrate progress and achievements. This can build confidence and motivation to continue embracing change. Celebrating progress reinforces positive behavior and encourages further growth.

Often times i find my clients and students suffering from creative blocks which hinder progress. Creative blocks need to be managed by engaging in creativity regularly. Foster creativity by engaging in regular creative activities. This can include artistic pursuits, problem-solving exercises, or other forms of creative expression. This should include discharging creativity in the myriad day-to-day aspects of life. Regular creativity helps maintain a flow of ideas and prevents blocks. At times a change of environment may also help to do so. A change of environment can stimulate creativity. Experiment with different settings or routines to overcome creative blocks. Changing your environment provides new stimuli and perspectives. You do so to ultimately seek inspiration. So always look for inspiration from various sources, such as books, art, nature, or conversations with others. Exposure to new stimuli can help reignite creativity. Seeking inspiration broadens your perspective and stimulates new ideas.

Although from a distance they seem to be different worlds the world of creativity and practicality must harmonize. And this balance has to be brought in by you through your Creative Psyche. Balancing creativity with practicality involves evaluating feasibility. Assess the feasibility of creative ideas and solutions. Consider factors such as resources, time, and potential impact to ensure practicality. Evaluating feasibility helps ensure that creative ideas can be effectively implemented. In addition, you must also always integrate practical considerations. Align creative solutions with real-world constraints and requirements. Ensure that creativity is balanced with practicality for effective implementation. Integrating practical considerations ensures that creative solutions are realistic and achievable. What you should not be afraid of here is seeking and receiving feedback. Obtain feedback from others to evaluate the practicality and effectiveness of creative ideas. Constructive feedback can help refine and improve solutions. Seeking feedback provides valuable insights and helps enhance creativity.

Doing all the above to cultivate and expand your Creative Psyche does take some time and effort but you do it anyhow because the returns are manyfold. What you get in return is bliss. What you get in return is a great distance from the woes and worries of your life. And that is what makes this all worth it.

Conclusion: The Creative Psyche as a Guiding Light

Creative Psyche, according to me and according to this book, manifests itself through a mindset and an attitude that is dedicated to seeking clarity about the true vision and purpose of life, which one can get closer to through absorbing instability and becoming stable first and still afterward, and most importantly living it. Creativity which is an essential skill for getting closer to such a mindset and an attitude is not only rare but more problematically lives only in the expectations of people or in the exceptions. Interestingly, intelligence, wisdom, common sense, and a few others also live in expectations or exceptions. Come to think of it we all expect such traits and attributes to be prevalent and universal but then they are not. And the place where you find them is exceptional and rare.

The creative psyche represents a transformative journey towards resilience and adaptability. By rewiring our psychological patterns and embracing creativity, we cultivate a mindset that thrives amidst instability. This shift enables us to absorb and integrate challenges, transforming them into opportunities for growth and innovation.

Embracing the creative psyche involves opening the mind to new experiences, developing flexibility, building resilience, and nurturing curiosity. It requires a willingness to challenge existing beliefs, experiment with new approaches, and view instability as a canvas for creativity.

As we navigate the complexities of modern life, the creative psyche serves as a guiding light, illuminating our path through uncertainty and change. It empowers us to approach challenges with curiosity, resilience, and a sense of wonder, transforming instability into a source of strength and growth. By embracing the creative psyche, we unlock our potential to thrive in an ever-changing world, finding stability not in the absence of change but in our ability to navigate it with grace and creativity.

11

FLOURISHING

The final chapter will explicate the concept of flourishing. Radioactive Flourishing is a positive construct that signifies the retention and expansion of well-being despite the presence of instability. It will summarize the many concepts discussed in the book and synthesize them to conclude the book.

Radioactive Flourishing is a combination of intention and ability of significantly absorbing the unabsorbable instability to reduce or eliminate the fall-out of radiation towards the self, and everything but the self. Flourishing is a state of being wherein an individual has identified meaning of life and has achieved enough security to be able to go and live out his or her purpose.

Flourishing is above and beyond the states of surviving and thriving. Flourishing is when an individual not only has attained the "freedom from" but also is aware and able to meaningfully engage in his or her "freedom to." Radioactive Flourishing is by no means a state of enlightenment or liberation or absolute Zen. Radioactive Flourishing is an enabler or a step forward in that direction.

Bear in mind that Radioactive Flourishing has two critical aspects to it. First is the expansion of the ability to absorb instability. My teacher's teacher used to say that often times you see a child crying because its balloon burst. A grandfather or a father or an uncle will come and give wisdom to the child that don't worry my child. It's just a balloon. For a balloon to burst is its core nature. We will get another one. The child still cannot come to terms with the loss of a balloon. Now the child does not have the wisdom to understand that it's just a balloon and hence is unable to absorb the instability. The same uncle or grandfather despite having the wisdom and being actively imparting it to the child is very next day brimming with instability because a balloon burst in the stock market. The uncle or the grandfather is unable to absorb

DOI: 10.4324/9781032627564-11

that instability and is becoming radioactive. So here what is key is the expansion of the ability to absorb any and every kind of instability that is directed towards you. The uncle or grandfather laughs at the inability of the child to absorb the instability originating from a burst balloon. But they themselves too cannot handle their respective burst balloon. Hence, the expansion of the ability to absorb instability is the first critical aspect of Radioactive Flourishing. My teacher is Swami Parmatmananda Saraswati, and his teacher was Swami Dayananda Saraswati.

Second critical aspect is that when you absorb a lot, you eventually also become highly radioactive. In other words, you become even more dangerous. Smaller fits of anger and lashing out are hurtful and unpleasant but they are not as harmful as a major fallout with an explosion impacting many others. So, the constant intentionality and goal of flourishing is substantially significant here. The instability is absorbed not to gather and become more lethal than before. The instability is absorbed so as to not pass it on to others and despite it flourish. Flourishing involves the actualization of the core essence of an individual's purpose through acceptance and excellence. Flourishing involves the equanimous prospering of all individual faculties and proclivities. Flourishing is not a channeled or a focused existence. Flourishing is an unhinged manifestation and realization. Flourishing is the inundation in compassion and a stark departure from singularly benefitting passions.

i will caution you about one thing though that as you get better at absorbing instability, the desire to test one's limits and abilities of absorbing instability is real and heavy. This is a risk and a slippery slope. You are not to actively seek instability and absorb it, because it is neither the goal nor the need. If instability somehow finds you (and most likely it will), then you should have the ability to absorb it. Before instability absorption, you must also try and get slightly better at instability avoidance. Being radioactive, we cultivate a potential to ruin, destroy, and devastate but we avoid doing any of the above because we simultaneously develop the ability to absorb it without imbibing it. So, it is ideally best to avoid it altogether.

One of the things that sows the seed of instability avoidance as well as flourishing in humans is their "Sarvangin Vikas." Sarvangin means holistic or comprehensive. And Vikas means progress or development or growth. For such growth and development, an individual needs to be exposed and trained in compassion for all his or her faculties. Of course, this can get elaborate and complex but here i will start with something simple and easy. i refer to it as the Triad Test.

Before i tell you more about the Triad Test, let me share with you the source from where the inspiration for it originated. It was in July 2021, while attending an exceptionally well-organized one-week conference on Creative Leadership. Creative Leadership was supported by its parent organization called Initiatives of Change (IofC) Switzerland. IofC Switzerland's vision is a just, peaceful, and sustainable world in which people act from a sense of global interdependence and responsibility. Overall IofC exists to Inspire, Equip, and Connect individuals with their inner voice to strengthen the moral and spiritual fabric of the individual and the world. Creative leadership was and will remain a very high-impact program for me for several reasons. The first and foremost being that it was entirely conceptualized and organized by a bunch of young adults from all over the world. They managed to start everything on time and end it on time as well. A remarkable feat in my humble opinion. They managed to gather participants from 75 countries. The Creative Leadership Conference addressed four themes, and i will provide a little description of each of the theme as shared by the bright youngsters of Creative Leadership.

1 Facing Uncertainty—Starting by acknowledging the problem's existence, we begin by accepting something must change.
2 Holding the Troubles—Instead of running from the chaos and uncertainty, we stay with the issue and sit with it.
3 Transforming Fear into Hope—We begin the process of changing our negative emotions into a new outlook.
4 Hope and Possibility—We leave seeing new possibilities and ideas for how to move forward.

It was during the second theme of Holding the troubles session that we, the participants, did this exercise. We were asked to move into the exercise with the assumption that we don't have answers. Assuming this we were asked to examine two questions: 1) What does it mean to listen deeply? 2) How can we care for ourselves? The guiding seed for the exercise was that this exercise is not about overcoming, which makes sense because we have already assumed that we do not have any answers. More importantly, this was about merely staying and being with the prevailing uncertainty in our respective lives. An inaugural attempt was to be made to find fruitful creativity in times of darkness. And a link between inner and outer listening and sustainable wholehearted involvement in the inner change-making was to be discovered and worked upon. We were asked to think and share with a group with a focus on thoughts, feelings, emotions, physical sensations/reactions, and more.

My learning from the session was that everyone is highly disembodied, and this disembodiment must be fought against. It is only through defeating the disembodiment that embracing the duality of a perceived troubled reality and hidden peaceful existence is possible. This exercise was, for me, about resolving a paradox that is very integral to us.

The triad is made up of head, heart, and body. As depicted in my notes below, i realized that i conducted my life dominated tremendously by my head. My thoughts dominated by existence. My heart did make a guest appearance from time to time with my emotions and feelings. And my body was edited out from the entire production. i realized that i ignored my body and did not do anything that was needed for it or inspired by it. This was and to a large extent still remains a source of instability. The path to flourishing is through harmonizing the triad. The moderator had said that we need to decolonize the rule of head over our hearts and body. And based on the pyramid you can clearly see what my state was back then (Figure 11.1).

For Sarvangin Vikas or flourishing, the pyramid has to change. It needs to be a perfect square. Any deviation from it being a perfect square is an indication of an imbalance. A harmonious balance as depicted in the square below where our thoughts, emotions, feelings, reactions, and physical sensations are all given equal weightage and inspire us similarly is what needs to happen for flourishing. The Triad test is a simple question followed by a quick analysis and decision-making (Figure 11.2 and Table 11.1).

Every individual has the ability developed and enhanced through inner listening to objectively assess if a given activity or endeavor is good or not for the three levels. Playing a video game can be good for the mind but not necessarily for the body. Similarly, there are many activities that are skewed towards the heart and not the head and body. Upon asking the question, an answer will emerge. Put it in the table in the right column.

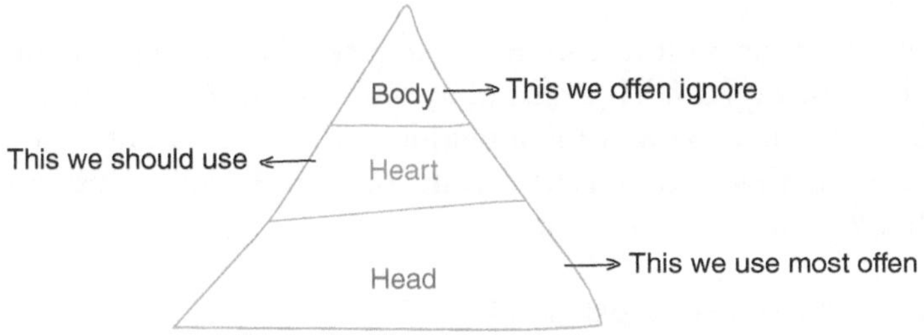

FIGURE 11.1 Pyramidal Structure of Head, Heart, Body.

FIGURE 11.2 Square Structure of Head, Heart, Body.

TABLE 11.1 Triad Test

Triad test Question: Is this activity or endeavor good for my Head, my Heart, and my Body?		
	Yes	*No*
Head		
Heart		
Body		
Outcome & Decision		

If you get 3 Yes, then don't hesitate to participate in the activity.

If you get 2 Yes, and 1 No, then consider and contemplate deeply if this activity has the potential to transform into 3 Yes. If there is a possibility, then go for it.

If you get 1 yes, and 2 No, then this activity is not sustainable and hence you should steer clear of it.

If you get 3 No, then just forget about it. This activity or thought is a useless and toxic pursuit.

Cultivating Intention

Flourishing is about both intention and ability. Cultivating intention is the first step because one can have the ability and still not flourish if he or she is lacking the intention. Now if the intention is there, the ability is developed soon after. So, in this section, i share with you four Aagrahas (meaning given below) that you must be aware of.

Aagraha is "persistent insistence."

Aagraha occurs in many contexts and my favorite is in the context of meals. For those who have experienced Indian *aagraha* know it far too well. The unending persistent affectionate insistence on eating more. And for those who haven't experienced it yet, they ought to visit their nearest Indian friend to experience a piece of this loving heaven. However, this is not one of the four aagrahas. This is just a little deviation from the main topic. But before we come back to the main topic, let me briefly mention the one form of aagraha that is globally popular.

Satyagraha is a form of *aagraha*, which is much more globally popular than the ones i am going to mention consecutively. *Satyagraha* is the persistent insistence of truth and absolute truth. Mohandas Karamchand Gandhi (Mahatma Gandhi) was the champion of Satyagraha. He used it as his primary weapon against the British to further his cause of obtaining India's freedom. Satyagraha has since been adopted by many great leaders of the world.

Now let me introduce to you four *aagrahas*, which are excellent means of fostering intention for flourishing. Their significance in an individual's life is immediate and substantial.

Snehaagraha

Snehaagraha makes others' heart a better place to live in and be a part of.

Love and compassion towards all living beings and things is Snehaagraha. We have become choosy and picky, and sadly really narrow about distributing our love and compassion. Our love and compassion should not be limited only for the ones that love us or think highly of us. Our love and compassion should be the same towards our hater and lover.

Love and compassion do not deplete upon giving. They are unlimited. i also want to acknowledge that *Snehagraha* is just as difficult as Satyagraha. We have to fight our own vulnerabilities, fear, and ego to persistently insist on equally loving and being compassionate towards everyone.

Sevaagraha

"Sevaagraha makes our soul a better place to live in and be a part of."

We are all conscious of our jobs but not of service. A job is a fulfillment of a duty in exchange of a reward, mainly monetary. Whereas service is the fulfillment of perceivable gaps in our surroundings, which are also a part of our duties that are discharged in exchange for nothing. Selfless service invites delight. Delight is pure joy, which is unbroken, unconditional, and unaccompanied. Something impossible to get from a job.

Aagraha or the persistent insistence for selfless servitude is scarce in today's society. What is mostly observed is its corrupt cousin. The version where *seva* serves a self-serving purpose or helps you create an attractive packet. Seva to yourself, Seva to uplift your body, seva to uplift your soul, seva to your place of residence, seva to your society, seva to your fellow living beings, seva to the planet are all forms of servitude that we must persistently insist in our lives.

Swachhatagraha

"Swacchatagraha makes our world a better place to live in and be a part of."

There are two spaces which Gods are willing and ready to accept it as their abode. The first is where women are respected and treated with dignity, and second is in spaces where cleanliness is prevalent. i don't feel the need to elaborate on the former because if you still haven't gotten it, then all i have for you is my love and compassion but no respect or regard.

Talking about the latter one, I feel that mankind has done a decent job of keeping his or her house clean and in some localities even their surroundings clean. But the surroundings of a major portion of humanity are unclean, unkempt, and dirty. We must expand our scope of influence when it comes to *Swacchata* (cleanliness). And without persistent insistence or *swacchata-graha*, we are doomed to be dwarfed by the ever-growing mountains of waste and filth.

Swamaanagraha

"Swamaanagraha makes your body a better place to live in and be a part of."

Self-respect is the first step to humility and humility is the first step to *moksha (salvation)*. Before you reach a stage where humility becomes your second nature and your ego has little to no effect on you, you must first extend yourself the due respect that you deserve.

Your respect for yourself should not be derived from you merely existing or being a member of some modern-day clan. It should instead be derived from acting (karma) on the path of righteousness (dharma). This is not to preach you on dharma and karma but to reach out to my friends and acquaintances who are struggling with self-worth, self-dignity and self-respect issues and have a really hard time thinking highly of themselves. To them, i say this seek your self-respect and dignity in your actions while pursuing the path of righteousness. You are not alone. You have well-wishers and advocates that are tirelessly following their path of righteousness and one day, hopefully soon, both the paths will merge.

Aagraha, once again, is persistent insistence. Sneha (love), Seva (service), Swacchata (cleanliness), and Swamaan (dignity) are waiting for your persistent insistence. As you engage with this, the intentionality portion of flourishing will automatically emerge from within you and start blossoming. The blossoming intentionality is a great blessing and a step towards flourishing. When you love, you embrace and accept, when you serve, you give unconditionally, when you engage in cleanliness, you remove a lot of filth and garbage from your physical and metaphysical surrounding, and when you start respecting yourself, you don't regress. Hence, i say to you, be not fearful to persistently insist.

How to Absorb Radioactivity

The ability to absorb radioactivity is increasingly significant if we want to restore peace, sanity, normalcy, and even a greater sense of civility. If people will continue to remain unable to absorb radioactivity, then we will continue to have clashes and skirmishes and sometimes outright violent conflicts. Unless we are able to keep certain biases, beliefs, emotions, in check we will keep stirring the pot. So here i give you insights on how one can navigate challenging and destabilizing situations through elevating selected abilities within using certain labels as frameworks. This approach employs the principles of Vivek (Discernment), a holistic understanding of Maryada (social and personal boundaries) and being aware of raag (attachment) and Dvesha (aversion).

Employing Vivek: The Power of Discernment

Vivek means the ability to discern. Discernment involves the ability to discriminate. As one becomes more in tune with his or herself, they cultivate the ability to discern. This ability to discern can be and should be put to use in understanding the difference between the true nature and the superimposed nature of things and beings. Vivek does not come easy because it is fogged by attachment, ego, emotions, and ignorance. In destabilizing situations or encounters or even emotionally charged situations, having a strong sense of Vivek will allow you to assess and analyze the root cause with unparalleled clarity. Vivek makes things clear and when things are clear nothing is hidden or obfuscated. This state of clarity instantly brings stillness and absorption of the unstability. There is an incredible text called Vivekchudamani, which elaborates on the characteristics, need, and application of Vivek. A must read I say. A few preliminary things that can be done to begin your journey into cultivating and developing Vivek are to seek guidance and knowledge from mentors, guides, and spiritual leaders who can instill indifference through enlightenment in you. You must also set time aside for introspection and study of the self to look at your values, your external and internal influencers, and how they instigate different thoughts, actions, and decisions through you. You must also practice the art of responding instead of reacting. Response is a prepared state whereas reaction is an unprepared state, and as noted in an earlier chapter, an unprepared individual is a big danger to society.

Considering Maryada: Setting Boundaries and Understanding Limitations

Maryada refers to both boundaries and limitations. Maryada can be the ethical and moral boundaries we set for ourselves and our interactions with others. We all operate within these boundaries for a harmonious and peaceful co-existence. And understanding and respecting these boundaries is crucial in preventing unstability, toxicity, and radioactivity. But the one nuanced meaning of Maryada that is often forgotten or missed out entirely is limitation. Limitations are where the eligibility or the ability of an individual stop. For example, a limitation of humans is to not being able to fly. Birds can fly but humans cannot. Similarly, within humans, we all have different limitations, which are also known as Maryada. Often times we ask why does this person have to behave erratically all the time. Well, the answer is that the manifestation of such behavior is that person's limitation. In most cases we see that people try to change for good but are simply unable to do so. This is due to their limitations. To overcome limitations is not only a challenging task but it also requires you to win over your own self, senses, and pleasures. Now this is difficult. The reason why gym memberships reduce greatly by 15th January is because of limitations. In the excitement of the new year, you may start something new but to keep it going requires overcoming your limitations and most people are unable to do so. It's like shining shoes. When you shine them, they look nice and clean and shiny but by the days end they lost their luster. Electrons when charged with energy jump their orbits but then their natural propensity is to return to their orbits. Similarly, people with their limitation of not being able to exercise daily will return to the same routine of neglecting their health and not exercising.

So, boundaries and limitations both make up Maryada. The way it helps in absorbing radioactivity is by helping an individual with a perspective behind why an individual is behaving the way he or she is behaving. Often time many people keep testing their partners in a relationship and they themselves don't like it either but their limitation stems from their insecurity and they are simply unable to overcome their insecurity, so they are compelled to repeat an unpleasant behavior again and again. Just as how i mentioned earlier in another example that my aunt was simply not able to take care of herself as proactively as my uncle did of himself and wanted her to do as well. It was her Maryada. If my uncle had understood that it was her Maryada and accepted it as is, much of the radioactivity would have been absorbed. The ignorance of other people's Maryada and the unconditional acceptance of it is what is the root cause of radioactivity. Once this can be understood and practiced, radioactivity can be absorbed, and behavior explosions can be brought down.

The key here is to know your boundaries and limitations and persistently strive to learn about other people's limits as well. Just as you have limits, others do too. Know them acknowledge them and work with them to foster healthy relations. The other important thing is also to know very well what you can tolerate and how much. This knowledge allows you to escape or eschew any situations where your boundaries are tested. If everyone deploys Vivek to understand and learn about their own and others' boundaries and limitations, the world will inherently be a less destabilizing place.

Attachment and Aversion

Our attachments and aversions are like what a slope is to water. Water flows rapidly on a slope. Our behaviors and reactions also just occur based on our attachments and aversions. i would like to remind you about the zone of unawareness here from an earlier chapter. Much of our likings and disliking are stored deep within that zone of unawareness. They cloud our judgment or in other words discernment and amplify emotional reactions or otherwise referred to as radioactive outbursts. By becoming fully aware of our attachments and aversions, individuals can mitigate their influence on decision-making. What would be ideal would be to become indifferent to both. Neither should attachments drive you nor should your aversion for someone or something make you do things. The balance is in indifference to both and rising above emotional feelings and outbursts. There is a lot more to be written about this, even an entire book or multiple volumes of books can be written about attachment, detachment, and aversion. But for us at this stage, being aware about them and how they nudge and stimulate us is important. The rest of the journey, i leave it to the curiosity of the reader to pursue and follow but i do want to leave you with one example and the example is that of a Coolie or a porter.

The Indifference of a Coolie

To learn about attachment and detachment and likes and versions a porter or a coolie is a great example. There is such a big lesson to learn from the life of a Coolie, especially his work and his work ethic. Often times we start associating and connecting our identity with our work, with the projects that we do, and we claim that we are awesome amazing and wonderful in case if we accomplish that work or project.

Now i want you to think about a coolie a porter who lifts your luggage. A Coolie lifts so much luggage every day and invariably multiple times a day. That's equivalent to doing multiple projects in a day. Now despite doing those multiple projects, a Coolie is not in any way attached or averse to the weight of the burden that he is carrying. A Coolie never gets any form of identity, purpose, or attachment towards the burden that he carries. People who work in the corporate sector, especially they start attaching themselves to their burden and it manifests in their communication styles, their management styles, their leadership styles. Getting attached to the burden of the task or the project that you carry is extremely counterproductive in the long run because when you get attached to it and if you have to move on or if you are made to move or if you are fired, it is really hurtful at a personal level when that burden goes away.

The going away of the burden causes a vacuum, which remains as a source of stress and anxiety for many. Their sense of doership that they ran the project, or it was their project keeps the wounds alive. And their hurt ego is also the reason why they keep doing some of the things over and over again, which are not good, which are not nice, which are very toxic at times so indulging in such behavior where you get attached to the burden that you carry is not worth it.

It is important to learn this from a Coolie. A Coolie never gets attached to the burden that he carries. He forgets about it the moment he drops it and moves on to the next burden. There is no recollection and there is no affinity. There is no attachment to the previous burden. This approach is the healthy approach. And i hope that many of you will take this seriously and apply to reduce instability in your life to avoid being a radioactive leader or team member. A radioactive leader or a team member proves to be counterproductive in the long run. A Coolie is what we always need to remember. The same can be said about a taxi driver or a rickshaw driver as well. Their level of detachment is envious and should be remembered and harnessed to rise above our own versions of attachments and aversions.

Harnessing Will and Resolve

Iccha Shakti (willpower) and Sankalp Shakti (resolve) are essential energies that can help in navigating life's challenges. Both are needed to overcome the barriers of limitations and ignorance. Without these two a stalemate sort of a situation persists. By focusing on these powers, one can approach situations with determination, purpose, and a balanced healthy outlook that is a cushion against unstability. The intentions need to be set right. They need to be clearly defined in the context of what we want to achieve. In this case it is the flourishing that we want to achieve. You can use some modern-day techniques such as manifestation and visualization to see yourself flourishing. It surely helps. You can also visualize yourself as an unperturbed absorptive being that is dedicated and committed to flourishing. For this, you must also regularly reaffirm your intentions to maintain focus and determination.

Keeping the Sense of Doership in Check

The sense of doership, or ego is solely responsible for obfuscating the truth and submerging us in an illusory existence. I and mine that emerge from the toxic sense of doership is contrary to flourishing. I am doing this. I have done this. This is mine. This belongs to me. Without me, all this would not have been possible. It's only me who is keeping this relation alive. Such statements and versions of it are all coming from a place of ego. Until and unless the ego is in check, flourishing is a distant dream. I say this because there is no real flourishing in ignorance. Just as there is no relevance of the palaces that you build in your dream in real life similarly as long as you keep living in ignorance there is no flourishing. You cannot escape harsh weather in the palaces of your dream. You cannot enjoy any luxury in those palaces either. They are nothing but trivializing illusions submerging us in the sea of ignorance.

By relinquishing excessive or in fact any attachment to this sense of doership, one can foster a flourishing mindset. i had mentioned earlier that thousands of accidents happen every day. None of them bother us but if an accident happens to anything related to me, I or mine that's where the problem starts.

Here are some very preliminary techniques to manage the Sense of Doership. The first and foremost thing that you can practice is surrender. Recognize that nothing is within your control; this means that you are also not the one doing. You are the one merely following. This reduces our attachment to the done. Practicing surrendering the done and the outcomes to a higher power or the flow of life helps in keeping ego in check. The other thing is to engage yourself in unconditional service. Engaging in unconditional service will shift focus from self to others. This can happen in the best way possible only through acts of service, which can help diminish the ego's hold on your psyche. What also needs to be integrally cultivated is gratitude. Nobody can achieve anything alone. You are always supported in ways that you sometimes are aware of and other times unaware of. Hence, i say acknowledge contributions from others and the universe to foster a deep sense of interconnectedness and dependence. When you are dependent your ego is naturally in check. It is only where you are living in the belief that you are independent; the problems begin preventing you from flourishing.

Navigating life's challenges, such as absorbing radioactivity and being in constant pursuit of flourishing, requires a blend of discrimination, boundary-setting, awareness of emotional tendencies, harnessing inner strength, and managing the sense of doership. By incorporating these principles into daily life, individuals can create a resilient and flourishing Creative mindset that allows them to effectively absorb and transform negative experiences into opportunities for growth. In this way, one can foster a deeper sense of peace and well-being, even in the face of adversity.

Where are Humans Living in the 21st Century?

This is a question; i was not sure if i should include in the first chapter or the final one. What choice i made must be obvious. The reason i chose to include this in the final chapter is because i wanted to be crisp about it and not too elaborate. In pursuit of crispness, i decided to bring in the normal curve to help me. The normal curve is a diagrammatic representation of the distribution of a given population. It is typically used in statistics to look at how the research samples' scores are distributed. Based on my informal survey, observations, and interactions, i can convincingly surmise that humans would be distributed as shown in the diagram below.

A large majority of humans are living in the surviving zone, where they are barely surviving. Those in really dire situations are included in this too.

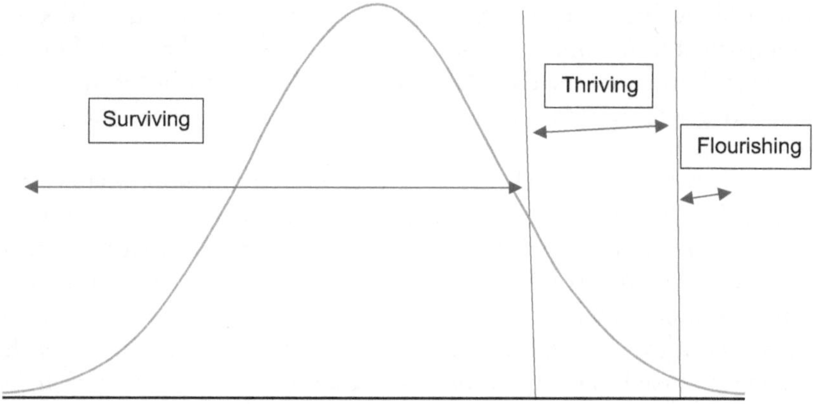

FIGURE 11.3 Normal Curve of People Surviving, Thriving, and Flourishing.

Survival can have a little bit of a spectrum depending on the having or not having of possessions. But here the mere fact that they are alive and are expected to remain alive gets them included in it. Almost 70% of humans fall in this category. A much smaller percentage of people in the range of 27% fall in the range of thriving. Thriving is a bit better than surviving but as far as I am concerned, it is a binary where surviving plus thriving is one category making up 97% of the humanity. Only 3% live somewhere in the zone of flourishing (Figure 11.3).

Flourishing is the most desired category and unlike the financial inequity much easier to equalize. In this case it is very easy to skew the normal curve into a curve where a large majority of humanity is flourishing. Flourishing does not require any material possessions or acquisitions. To flourish one cannot go anywhere. One can flourish where they are. One can flourish whether they are rich or poor. To flourish one also does not need to acquire or possess anything material or physical. Just because you are a doctor or an engineer or a president, you are not flourishing. You can be a mendicant and still be flourishing because this flourishing is behavioral flourishing. It is also perpetual and not ephemeral. My hope with the work in this book is that less and less folks are impacted by instability. My goal is not to influence radioactivity. Destabilizing agents are only going to increase with the passage of time as noted in the first chapter. So, what we can do is to bring a change at our end. Radioactive flourishing is that change in a person where instability is absorbed.

Final Message

Flourishing is when you are existing without expectation. Flourishing is a state wherein you fully realize the significance of your human birth, which is extremely and incredibly rare as well as precious. Once this realization dawns in, many of the unnecessary and ephemeral pursuits start seeming to be meaningless and not worth one's time. In the same breath, i can also say that all of the instability that comes to a person also becomes insignificant and because of this insignificance, it loses its ability to influence and overpower you. In the state of flourishing your focus is constantly inward and away from the world that is perceived and experienced through the senses. In other words, in the flourishing state the zone of unawareness that exists within and manifests mysteriously is dissolved. Once any human being is able to realize the illusory nature of the instabilities his ability to absorb the radioactivity becomes unparalleled. All the pain, misery, irritations, troubles dissolve in water like salt in water. Flourishing is not a physical condition. Flourishing is a cognitive attitude. Flourishing is a state of understanding and clarity where the radiations around you don't bother you anymore. Just as the sun does not get bothered by the temporary gathering of clouds that eclipse its effect and impact. Similarly, a human being too in flourishing mode does not get bothered by the temporary ebbs and flows of radiations, uncertainties and instabilities around him or her or them.

Flourishing also refers to a state of being where you are fully aware that while nothing belongs to you, you still are everything. This might seem a bit contradictory or confusing, but it is the most reformed state of cognitive clarity. When you are everything, nothing is anything else and, in this oneness, both the stability as well as the instability are absorbed and canceled out. When a material in this case a human being remains perpetually in a stable state then his or her actions and thoughts and decisions are not going to be of a radioactive nature where they negatively hurts and harm the people around. There is no radioactive leak from within the system. There is no fallout.

The ultimate flourishing is in the precise knowing of the "i" by a process of systematic separation from "my." And for that one has to ensure that Dharma ki Jay ho, Adharma ka Naash ho, Praaniyo me sadbhaav ho, Gau Mata ki Raksha ho, Om Kar ka Jaap ho, and Moksha ki iccha ho. In other words, your duties become important to you, you repel unrighteousness, you live in synergy and harmony with all living beings, you care and protect cows that nourish us with their milk like our mothers, you constantly are reciting and thinking of your almighty, and lastly there arises a desire for liberation in you. When we are able to absorb instability and still remain stable, we become the true champions of the very nature of the cosmos which is perennial, pure, and truthful.